Just-In-Time Purchasing:

In Pursuit of Excellence

Just-In-Time Purchasing:

In Pursuit of Excellence

PETER L. GRIECO, JR.

MICHAEL W. GOZZO

JERRY W. CLAUNCH

PT PUBLICATIONS, INC.
653 MAIN ST.
PLANTSVILLE, CT 06479

Also available from PT Publications, Inc.

MADE IN AMERICA: *The Total Business Concept*
SUPPLIER CERTIFICATION: *Achieving Excellence*
BEHIND BARS: *Bar Coding Principles and Applications*

First Printing   **May 1988**
Second Printing   **June 1989**

Library of Congress Cataloging in Publication Data

Grieco, Peter L., 1942-
  Just-in-time purchasing.
  Bibliography; p. 191.
  Includes index.
  1. Purchasing. I. Gozzo, Michael W., 1939-
II. Claunch, Jerry, 1947- . III. Title.
HF5437.G74 1988   658.7'2   88-5802
ISBN 0-945456-01-8

TABLE OF CONTENTS

PREFACE

At a time when costs related to purchasing account for over 50% of the total cost of a product, it would be wise to pay attention to the procurement role in your company. Paying attention may even be vital when one considers the effects of domestic and global competition.

Purchasing has become increasingly important and because of that, there is an urgent need to rethink the way one conducts the business of procurement. That is the focus of this book — showing how to effect the transition from Purchasing as a department of clerical paper-shufflers to an integral department involved in the planning, marketing, design, engineering, production and quality control functions of a company. In short, Purchasing must come to adopt the philosophy of Just-In-Time (JIT) and Total Quality Control (TQC) or, what we call, the Total Business Concept (TBC).

This transition is possible and we have written this book to show you not only how to implement JIT Purchasing, but how to do it in America. We believe that American companies are capable of changing without resorting to Far Eastern solutions. We have seen it happen here; we hope to show you how to become competitive by drawing on our significant level of experience with companies like Apple Computer, Kawasaki, Digital Equipment Corporation, Computervision, General Foods, Cosmair, Allied Signal and others.

WHAT IS JIT PURCHASING?

<u>JIT Purchasing is the uninterrupted flow of 100% acceptable materials delivered on due dates, at optimal cost, 100% of the time.</u>

Why strive for anything less? We aren't saying that you will get there in one quarter or one year. We are saying that if you don't set the above conditions as a goal and strive for continuous improvement, then you won't even have the luxury of maintaining your present position. You will begin to slide backwards. Many American and foreign companies already subscribe to the definition above and are enjoying the lower costs and increased profits which ensue. And if your competition is not embarking on a JIT Purchasing program, you can be sure that they will be very shortly. It is too costly *not* to begin.

If there is an urgency to the form of our message, it does not carry over into the contents. We don't believe in quick fixes based on technology or software. They are tools to use, certainly, but only in the sure and steady process toward more effective management. This is where the problem lies. Any other method simply treats the symptoms and does not cure the disease. That is why we so strongly prescribe the adoption of a mind-set which is proactive, not reactive.

We deem critical: Supplier Partnerships, Total Cost, Total Quality Control and the Theory of One. These are the four beams which will support the entire structure.

1. <u>Supplier Partnerships</u>. In JIT Purchasing, it is far more profitable and reliable to develop long-term relationships with suppliers in which they are partners, not victims. This necessitates a level of trust and cooperation not usually found in today's business world. Long-term partnerships only work in two directions. If a supplier is shipping "zero-defect" material, he expects to receive engineering information and production schedules from your company which will help him in setting his own schedules. If he doesn't get your cooperation, he cannot maintain the quality standards you demand. Partnership comes through the implementation of a Supplier Certification program which seeks to educate and train suppliers in the necessity and virtues of process and quality controls in their facilities. The result is a "win-win" situation.

2. <u>Total Cost Approach</u>. A prevailing thought today is that we must raise the selling price of products in order to maintain profits while costs rise.

Unfortunately, this can lead to a never-ending spiral upwards. When I increase my price, your costs go up. So, you raise your price and eventually that makes my cost go up and so on. JIT Purchasing, however, takes this equation and looks at it in another way.

Instead of constantly revising selling prices upward, we begin by setting the selling price based on total cost and a fair profit. Now, if we find our profit shrinking because costs are rising, we don't change the selling price. What does that leave if we still want to maintain a fair profit? Costs. We keep the selling price and profit the same by attacking and reducing all the costs incurred while making a product.

Total costs are those costs incurred by the whole company in manufacturing a product. Some of these costs are apparent and some are hidden. Current accounting methods tend to depend on price analysis which uses the seller's price without examining or evaluating the separate elements of cost and profit.

3. <u>Total Quality Control</u>. Purchasing has a unique role to play in this area. Many of the factors which influence quality at supplier's facility, such as lead time, set-up reduction, Statistical Quality Control, Supplier Certification Programs and supplier "zero-defect" programs should be the responsibility of Purchasing since they are responsible for supplying the right material at the right time in the right place in the right quantity. This puts a premium on making sure that the material is always free of defects. The JIT environment functions with a minimum of inventory from which workers can take good parts when they must scrap a bad part. Therefore, Purchasing must help to implement a quality control program within the company as well as with suppliers so that production lines do not come to a halt because their process is out of control or because they are receiving bad parts. Like other JIT actions, quality improvement is an on-going activity. If it stops, then you stop improving.

4. <u>Theory of One</u>. The Theory of One states that an operator on a line obtains only as much material as he or she needs to make one product. It is based on a "pull" system of manufacturing where the act of pulling material triggers replenishment, much like the Kanban system which you have read much of lately. A "pull" system, as opposed to a "push" system, works in conjunction with

the components above. Purchasing's job in this streamlined environment is to insure that stock levels are replenished as needed and accurately reflect customer demand. You should not be told "to make and hold inventory."

All these areas are the basis of JIT Purchasing and are the focus of this book. Our chapter headings are indicative of how we apply these ideas. Purchasing must act in concert with other departments. If Supplier Partnerships, the Total Cost Approach, Total Quality Control and the Theory of One are the building blocks of JIT Purchasing, then team-building and interdepartmental cooperation are the driving forces behind the Total Business Concept. It won't be easy, but it can be done. We have seen it happen here in America.

Peter L. Grieco, Jr.
Michael W. Gozzo
Jerry W. Claunch

ACKNOWLEDGEMENTS

With each book, we become more firmly convinced of the importance of the three-part experience upon which we draw — teaching, consulting and "real-world" practice in manufacturing. To those who have participated with us in these three endeavors, we give our most sincere thanks for the education and training you have provided us. Thank you for showing us that the Total Business Concept is truly a process undertaken by a team. Once again, we would like to thank Steven Marks for his editorial assistance in making our ideas appear on these pages. We would also like to express our appreciation to our colleagues and staff at Professionals for Technology Associates, Inc. for their untiring support. Lastly, we wish to express our warmest thanks to our families who helped us to achieve our dreams.

CHAPTER ONE: The Role of Purchasing in the JIT/TQC Age

In some land, in some time long ago, the first manufacturer made plowshares in times of peace and swords in times of war. Material acquisition was not difficult. He located his factory near the sight where iron ore was mined and near a forest where fuel for his forge's fire could be obtained. He had a ready market and no great production planning problems. When he needed to switch his product line, he, of course, merely told his workers to beat the swords into plowshares. Since the material for either product was the same, most of his costs were paid out to skilled workers in metal.

Centuries later, a descendant of this first manufacturer made fine clothing for the ladies and gentlemen of his time. He had new machines which did much of the work formerly done by seamstresses, but he had some problems with material acquisition. He depended on a whaling fleet in his city to supply him with the rich fabrics that came from Europe. He needed to buy silk from an importer who brought the material from China. He even had to frequent the shop of a merchant who sold the mother-of-pearl buttons which had become a fashion rage of the time. The Industrial Revolution had certainly lowered the percentage of his labor costs in relation to his total costs, but he found the percentage of costs associated with procurement rose as the other fell.

Now we are in our century. A second Industrial Revolution has reduced, through the use of information and computers, costs associated with labor and operations still further. Our third manufacturer, who now makes lawnmowers, finds a situation in which material acquisition costs comprise over 80% of her total costs.

Quite obviously, departments who control purchasing and the management of material have an opportunity to contribute directly to the company's profit by reducing procurement costs as part of the company's total cost objectives. Manufacturers in the Far East have done just this, although it may not be readily apparent. This is because most news we receive emphasizes areas such as set-up reduction, production and inventory control, delivery, group technology, etc. without hardly mentioning the large role which Purchasing can and does play in Just-In-Time (JIT).

Purchasing, thus, has a new role in an age where a Total Business Concept is fast becoming the norm, and, even more importantly, a necessity for survival. What, then, is Purchasing's new role?

The role encompasses all that it was before and numerous more opportunities. Defining the "more" is the purpose of this book, but, in the meantime, let us define the nine guidelines which will help you visualize the scope of this new role. First, the definition:

> The role of Purchasing is to provide an uninterrupted flow of 100% acceptable materials on the due dates, at the optimal costs, 100% of the time.

The real surprise of this definition is that some people still think of Purchasing's duties as being merely clerical (order placers). To have that as Purchasing's principal role must surely come to an end. The future simply will not allow it. How we realize the activities of the definition above and how we fashion procurement's role in the future relies upon our ability to adopt and adapt the following guidelines to implement change:

GUIDELINES FOR PURCHASING'S NEW ROLE

1. **REVISIT THE TRADITIONS** — Ask yourself whether software, hardware and other equipment or new techniques truly contribute to the operating efficiency of the whole company. Strip away all wasteful and repetitive actions until you arrive at the core values and contributions of Purchasing.

2. **STRIVE TOWARD PROACTIVE SUPPLIER MANAGEMENT, NOT REACTIVE EXPEDITING** — The Purchasing Department aware of production schedules, supplier problems, financial considerations, sales forecasts, marketing research and customer needs — in short, company-wide goals — acts as a fire-preventer rather than a fire-fighter.

3. **REDEFINE THE SUPPLIER SELECTION CRITERIA** — The challenge is to select a qualified supplier early in the process. The objective in a certification program is to create a foundation upon which to build. A supplier who possesses all the right capabilities is more likely to become an excellent partner.

4. **DEVELOP LONG TERM RELATIONSHIPS WITH SUPPLIERS** — The myth is that Purchasing can only get the best price when suppliers bid in a competitive environment. The fallacy is that the best price does not always cost the company the least amount. Also, cost reductions come from focused Purchasing efforts.

5. **INTRODUCE SUPPLIER CERTIFICATION** — Hand in hand with supplier development, this guideline is one of the tenets of the Total Business Concept (TBC). There is a minimal effect by Purchasing if you don't attempt to establish a zero-defect program.

6. **TRAIN AND EDUCATE SUPPLIERS IN JIT/TQC** — The force behind supplier development and certification, training and education should not be restricted to your own company. As with any good educational experience, you may learn as much from your suppliers as you teach them.

7. **SPONSOR A SUPPLIER SYMPOSIUM** — Begin with "A" level items and invite those suppliers to visit your plant and see JIT/TQC in action. It is imperative that your company give up a "siege attitude" in which the supplier is viewed as an enemy bent on robbing you of money and trade secrets.

8. **MOVE TOWARD ELECTRONIC DATA INTER-CHANGE (EDI)** — This may seem to contradict the first guideline. If you look closer, however, we don't advocate throwing out the baby with the bathwater. Some technological innovations may help you reduce costs. EDI will help you achieve "paperless purchasing" as well as create an indispensable pool of common data.

9. **BECOME A "CHANGE AGENT" ON THE TEAM** — The Purchasing Department is not an island to itself. The company unable to embrace the future will be a remnant of the past. Purchasing needs to take a leadership role in JIT efforts.

Two themes run through this set of guidelines and, indeed, the whole book. First is the need for a company-wide perspective, rather than a narrow-minded departmental view. Second is the emphasis on costs, apparent and hidden. Once again, the manner in which costs affect the whole company, rather than the individual department. These two themes come together in the profit equation.

The prevailing thought in industry today is that the profit equation looks like this:

PROFIT = SELLING PRICE - COST

The company goal is to make a profit. In our efforts to attain this goal, we attempt to control costs. But, when they go up, we react by increasing the selling price. Our suppliers, of course, have the same goal and react in much the same way as we do. In such a situation, it is not surprising for costs to spiral upwards.

The thought in many Far Eastern companies and some U.S. companies is to put an end to this spiral and find another method. Indeed, this method allows everybody to come out on top when companies adhere to its basic supposition. That supposition is that the Selling Price is determined, set and controlled. If the Profit is not adequate, then Costs are attacked and reduced. The new equation looks like this:

SELLING PRICE = COST + PROFIT

We can no longer simply increase the selling price in response to falling profits or increasing costs. Our job is to reduce costs continuously by uniting Purchasing's efforts with the efforts of the entire company.

And *that job* is accomplished by the adoption of JIT/TQC. What is JIT/TQC? It is a philosophy for conducting business, what we refer to as a Total Business Concept (TBC) **(1)** which unites the two themes of cost reduction and company-wide participation noted above. It is an all-out commitment to the elimination of waste and the cultivation of quality and efficiency at every step.

In a certain sense, all business philosophies promise somewhat the same. TBC is different because it requires profound changes in the mind-set of the professional, whether that person is a chief executive officer, manager, supervisor or floor worker. JIT/TQC is like a map upon which you will draw your own individual routes. This may be upsetting to people who want and expect an "off-the-shelf" software system or a technological fix. But, because the routes will be your paths, adapted to the idiosyncrasies of your company, the chances for success are measurably greater. They are also greater if you are able to assimilate the following characteristics of a JIT/TQC mind-set:

THE MIND-SET OF A TBC PROFESSIONAL

1. Cultivate a "can-do" attitude
2. Believe in "small is beautiful"
3. Eliminate waste
4. Seek simplicity
5. Work for continuous improvement
6. Make success visible
7. Communicate

"Sure! Sure!," some of you are saying, "I can do that. All it takes is the of study Far Eastern philosophies."

Others are saying, "What do you want me to do? Sit on a mountain and contemplate my future? Where are the hard and cold facts?"

The hard and cold facts will come. Thinking that you have to stop being an American and change cultures will not help you achieve JIT/TQC. Let's turn now to what is true of the Japanese and much of the rest of the Far East. Philosophies similar to JIT/TQC were first implemented in Japan. Because of this fact, many people want to believe that the Oriental culture is what makes it work and that is why it won't work here.

The following are true of Japanese business philosophy:

1. Market share is more important than earnings.
2. The company president never hands orders down.
3. The Japanese prefer to be part of a group and use committees extensively.
4. Everyone, from top management to the rank and file, has input and becomes involved before implementation.
5. Decisions are made after all persons involved are contacted and all information is shared. Implementation then proceeds quickly.
6. The Japanese are slow to make a decision. Once made, however, it is "cast in bronze".
7. The maximum size of a unit within a company is 300 people.
8. They do have lifetime employment. However, it exists mostly at large corporations.
9. There is tremendous pressure to succeed in school. Tutoring begins before kindergarten.
10. There is less vertical integration in Japan. Much subcontracting occurs and when the work level slows, the subcontractor shuts down.
11. Company unions are not strong and work closely with management. Since they are not trade unions, crosstraining is used extensively.

The following is true in the Japanese workplace:

1. They have a sense of national purpose.
2. They have clear cut, realistic goals at the national level.
3. They are willing to do whatever they can to achieve those goals without compromising their ethics.
4. They are obsessed with productivity and take it personally.
5. They maintain a very low inventory level and take personal responsibility to maintain that level.
6. If a machine is about to break down, the worker stays

until the machine is repaired.
7. Suppliers know a missed delivery date is disastrous.
8. Competition is fierce. They will not stop for lunch and will work overtime without notice.
9. Parts received from suppliers are 100% good.
10. They do this without inspectors.
11. The operator has responsibility for quality.
12. The operator will stop if he/she cannot produce quality parts.
13. The Japanese employee realizes that absenteeism, strikes, etc. are to the detriment of the company. If the company does not make a profit, they won't profit either.
14. The Japanese do a better job at engineering.
15. They do a better job at supplier relations.
16. There is no jealousy about job descriptions.
17. They communicate better. They don't need computers.
18. They have a strong attitude toward cost improvement.

On our most recent fact-finding tour of the Far East, we toured the Toyota assembly facility in Toyota City. We observed that when the bell sounded for the afternoon break, employees did not drop everyting and run to a break area. In fact, workers were busy completing the operation at hand and getting components ready for when their break was over. We wonder how this would be accepted in North American plants.

There are certainly differences between American and Far Eastern attitudes to the operation of businesses, but there is nothing in the preceding lists which is exclusively Oriental in design or nature. What we keep coming back to is the attitude, the mind-set. The Japanese attitude to problem solving is different from American management's approach:

**WE TREAT THE SYMPTOM,
THEY CURE THE DISEASE.**

For example, if we have rejected parts, we rally to repair those parts. The Japanese put controls in place to prevent rejects.

At Brothers Manufacturing facility in Nagoya, Japan, when we asked a question about the level of supplier quality performance being less than 100%, the response was: "We are not allowed to think that way."

Furthermore, JIT/TQC does work in America. There is ample proof that it does. Consider the following examples:

AMERICAN MANUFACTURERS' EXPERIENCE WITH JIT/TQC

APPLE COMPUTER, MACINTOSH DIVISION
Inventory turns — 24 per year
More than 50% of suppliers were certified
Vendor base cut by over 50%

XEROX
Rejects on out-sourced parts from 5000 Parts per Million (PPM) to 1300 PPM

GENERAL FOODS
Inventory accuracy greater than 90%
Set-up time in manufacturing area reduced by more than 50%
Compliance to schedule showed 40% improvement

MOTOROLA
Reduced inventory by $210 million

GENERAL ELECTRIC, LEXINGTON
Productivity up by 20%

NUMMI, FREMONT, CA
Absenteeism, from 28% to 2%

HARLEY DAVIDSON
Cycle frame process time was cut from 72 days to 2 days
Set-up times reduced by 75%
Productivity up 30%
Inventory down by $22 million
Warranty costs down by 46%

KAWASAKI, Lincoln, Nebraska
Set-up time on punch press — 45 minutes to less than 1minute
Eliminated set-up on final assembly line
Implemented minimal spec prints
Achieved 26 inventory turns a year

FERRO MANUFACTURING COMPANY
Productivity up 46%
Scrap reduced 67%
Rework hours cut 93%
Total cost of quality down 47%
Assembly floor space 15% smaller
Operator monitors: schedule goals, efficiency, quality

STAR MANUFACTURING COMPANY
On-time deliveries up 30%
Cost of mis-fabrication, shortages, back orders cut 50%
Inventory year-end adjustments cut over 90%
Inventory turns from 2.3 to 9.0
Productivity increased 40%
Cycle times cut from 4 months to 4 weeks

ELECTROMECHANICAL EQUIPMENT MFG. CO.
Inventory turns doubled
Productivity up 30%
Out-going defects down 58%
Lead time from 21 days to 1 day

So it is possible for JIT/TQC to work in America. The above facts are hard and cold. On the other hand, the basic tenet of JIT/

TQC is a philosophy of *constant improvement*. The size of your percentages and the speed in which you obtain these benefits depends primarily on the desires, dedication and tenacity of management. There are several major areas to which you must attend.

The first area is orienting your thinking and your actions to a pull system of manufacturing rather than a push system. We are all familiar with push systems in which we push material and parts and sub-assemblies through a production line based on sales forecasts. Using production goals, developed from these forecasts, we then release to work centers based on their capacity to produce. We store materials needed to build our product in various inventories. And when we have completed production, we store the product in finished goods warehouse. We can't deny that this system works, in a fashion, but the question is whether or not it is the most efficient and cost-effective.

The answer is a clear "No!" A pull system, by starting at the other end of the production line, is far more efficient and reduces inventory considerably. In the ideal pull system, you should employ what we call the Theory of One. The Theory of One states that an operator on a line obtains only as much material as he or she needs to make one product. There is one operational rule to make this work and it is that the Act of Pulling Triggers Replenishment. In other words, a customer places an order for a lawnmower. The finished goods assembly receives the order and pulls one engine, one chassis and one handle assembly from the respective sub-assembly areas. Each of these sub-assembly areas must now replenish what has been pulled by finished goods assembly. Each one goes to their particular work centers and pulls the parts it needs to make an engine or a chassis. The work centers, in turn, pull from raw material or internal and/or external suppliers to replenish their area.

The whole effort can be likened to a magnet which pulls different parts to the point of sale while management insures that stocks are replenished to levels dictated by the pulling.

The second area to which management must give attention is quality. This is the area which has probably received the most attention, and rightly so, because of the work and writings of W.

Edwards Deming, J.M. Juran, Armand Feigenbaum and Philip B. Crosby. Each have taken a slightly different approach to quality, but there are certain dominant themes. Quality improvement is an on-going activity. If this activity stops, you stop improving.

For example, a pharmaceutical manufacturer asked us why he needed to chart numerous control points and what would he do with the output. Our response was that you can over-control processes and activities. The key is to chart the critical measurements first, correct the problems, then select a new set of critical measurements.

Another theme is the belief that if you are inspecting parts in your receiving departments, you have already lost the battle. Nothing less than defect-free parts from suppliers is acceptable. This obviously entails close relationships with them as we will discuss later. Yet another theme is the need for some type of statistical process control (SPC) which addresses process capability. Purchasing, of course, plays a leading role in achieving a "zero-defect" environment, but always in league with other departments and with suppliers.

Purchasing will also find itself involved in a third area, that of set-up reduction, lead time reduction and lot sizing. Purchasing's task, among many others in JIT/TQC, is to insure the delivery of the right quantity at the right time at the right total cost.

This means frequent, small deliveries directly to the production line in order to reduce inventories. To do so is of no value until the factory floor is able to wean itself from long production runs in favor of flexible manufacturing. In flexible manufacturing, machine operators must be able to reduce set-up time so that production can quickly change from producing one item to another. Ideally, the line should be able to run lot sizes of one so that first a sewing machine is made, followed by a typewriter, followed by another model or a different product. This is, indeed, the case at Brothers manufacturing plant in Japan.

But, Manufacturing is not going to employ flexible manufacturing, reduced lot sizes and set-up times if it feels that Purchasing can not guarantee reduced lead times and timely deliveries. It is something of a vicious circle which can only be broken by both

Manufacturing and Purchasing cooperating along with the supplier. This leaner style of operations is like a person trying to go on a diet. That person is not assured of success if the spouse and children eat chocolates and potato chips instead of carrots and celery sticks.

The fourth and last major area covers Purchasing's relationship with suppliers. Obviously much of your success depends upon the development of suppliers capable of meeting the demands of a JIT/TQC company. As we have already mentioned, this will require education and training on your part in order to teach them the new business philosophy. Ideally, you will be such a good teacher that your suppliers will see its value and implement the philosophy in their own companies. Underlying all this development is a close, mutually beneficial environment in which information is shared that many will see as a radical departure from the "us-against-them" mentality present now. Supplier development means *making the supplier a part of YOUR organization*. Develop suppliers for the life of the part or for the life of the company because as the quality goes up, the price comes down.

JIT/TQCers have a favorite cartoon which aptly demonstrates the focus of all their efforts to reduce waste. In the cartoon, we see a manufacturer sailing serenely across the water in a small boat. Far below him are creatures of the deep indicating the many and varied problems his company encounters. But, floating on a high level of inventory, these problems are not visible to him. Also in this cartoon, we see another manufacturer peering across his bow as his boat carefully maneuvers between the same monsters which now break the water's surface. This manufacturer has chosen to lower inventory levels so that it is able to see and then correct the problems the company encounters.

The point is that we can not, must not, compensate for problems, errors and sloppiness with solutions that hide the basic problems. JIT/TQC emphasizes producing exactly what is needed, precisely when it is required. It stimulates a quest for constant improvement through imaginative attention both to the overall task and to the details. In short, JIT/TQC seeks, through the development of true responsibility, authority and accountability, to make the operations, processes, etc. of your company truly visible. Because when they are visible, you can solve them. Imagine yourself having x-ray, telescopic, microscopic and bird's-eye vision all at the same time and you will get the idea of what JIT/TQC can do.

We think it is plain where our emphasis lies. Team-building and interdepartmental interaction are the primary driving forces behind JIT/TQC.

CHAPTER TWO: Concepts for the Transition Period

The rule for the transition to JIT/TQC Purchasing is this:

CLEAR THE COBWEBS,
SO YOU CAN SEE THE SPIDER WEB.

What do we mean by this? Imagine yourself in a room in a deserted house, perhaps even a house haunted by wasteful practices of the past. It is your job to clean up the mess. As you brush cobwebs from the corners of the room and off the furniture, you discover a network of lines. They are different from the tangle of strands, bearing clumps of dust, that have given the room an unorganized look.

This network, which is surprisingly strong and ordered, turns out to be a spider's web. For any of you who have seen a spider's web, beaded with dew, in the early morning light, you know what a beautiful sight you have uncovered. It is the beauty of organization, of simplicity and of elegance.

A spider's web has much in common with a well-organized company. What is most important about the web is its purpose. Whether the spider sits in the center or on the edges, the web's construction is such that a disturbance any where in the network reverberates throughout. This is how a well-managed company should be organized. This is Purchasing's goal — what the transition moves toward — a network of dependence and communication extending throughout the company and its suppliers.

The transition period is incomplete, if it merely concerns itself with considerations internal with the company. The poet, John Donne, once said that "no man is an island". The same can be said for companies. As for Purchasing, this primarily means a transition toward better relationships with suppliers and a recognition that the internal and external are integrally linked. Numerous companies overlook this partnership.

Thus, the spider web extends into the outside world, but here the analogy ends. For in JIT/TQC Purchasing, it is important not

to view your purpose as the spider views the web as a means to prey on unsuspecting insects. You aren't going to drain your suppliers dry and then roll them into silken bundles that will hang like trophies on your web. Your job will be to facilitate the movement of ideas and information from the inside of your plant to suppliers and vice versa. This will require seeing company operations in terms of function, rather than department.

Each department in a company normally has its own goals. We have identified them as follows:

TYPICAL U.S. MANUFACTURING CONCERNS BY DEPARTMENT

Manufacturing	**Manufacturing Engineering**
Work center efficiency	Manufacturability
High volume	Routing
Few set-ups	Production rates
Work force utilization	Simplicity
Productivity	Methodology

Quality Control
    Obtaining quality from
      suppliers
    Assurance of quality
      in process and finished
      goods

Production Scheduling
    Level schedule to
      manufacturing
    Responsive to sales
    Meeting timetables

Marketing
    Forecasting
    Market research

Accounting
    Compile information
    Report posture
    Profit and loss

Sales
    Goods availability
    Satisfaction of customer
    Achieving sales quotas

Design Engineering
    Design Quality
    Marketing acceptance
    Field service/Complaints
    Creativity

Inventory Control
    Turns
    Availability
    Minimizing investment

Purchasing
    Multiple sources
    Delivery
    Price
    Lead time

Even in a tightly organized and hierarchial company, these divisions between departments tend to blur. In a company employing a total business concept, they blur even further because it is more natural to group by function, rather than department. Quality, for example in the TBC environment, is the concern of all departments. It is a function that crosses over departmental line. In the preceding chapter, we said that JIT/TQC rests on the pillars of team-building and departmental interaction. What results from these premises is an organization based on function, rather than department.

JIT purchasing demands interdisciplinary cooperation. This is primarily due to the precision required in scheduling frequent, small deliveries and by the absence of excess inventories which puts a demand on defect-free parts. Thus, Purchasing must operate in an environment in which there is little room for wasteful mistakes. This necessitates gathering input from a number of departments and people in order to make sound procurement decisions.

For example, let's say that your company has decided to

change a model line. Under a departmental structure, Engineering Design works up plans based on data which Marketing has determined reflects future customer demand. Manufacturing Engineering then figures out ways to retool machines and perhaps reroute production lines. Production, then, decides on schedules partly based on forecasts drawn up by Sales. Finally, Purchasing gets the specifications and blueprints. You now find suppliers for volume production who can deliver the parts as ordered. Typically, engineering has sourced the initial parts from a prototype company.

Such a departmental attack on a company-wide problem is fragmented. We are reminded of a maze in which each department works in its own little cubicle and lobs hand grenades, or decisions, over the partitions to the department on the other side. In such an environment, it is not surprising for Purchasing to order a part, perhaps a one-inch screw, when a seven-eighths-inch screw, already stocked, could have been used. But, Engineering Design never asked Manufacturing if this was possible and nobody asked Purchasing about the availability. We must eliminate the lack of cooperation in our companies and organize each department to achieve the goal of satisfied customers.

This may be taking the case to an extreme, but it is clear that teamwork, the grouping together of various departments to achieve the fulfillment of each function, is vital to the success of JIT/TQC. In a functional structure, all the departments with an interest in a problem literally sit down at the same table and hash out a decision and the means to bring that decision to fruition. This arrangement can work on an ad hoc basis, but you may soon find that a restructuring of Purchasing may help to make the process of teamwork even more efficient.

One restructuring revolves around the concept of Materials Management. In their book, *Purchasing and Materials Management: Text and Cases*, authors Lamar Lee, Jr. and Donald W. Dobler define this concept as:

> "... a confederacy of traditional materials activities bound by a common idea — the idea of an integrated management approach to planning, acquisition, conversion, flow , and distribution of production materials from the raw material state to the finished-product state." **(1)**

They go on to say that under the aegis of materials management falls all the traditional activities of Purchasing, "plus all other major procurement responsibilities, including inventory management, traffic, receiving, warehousing, surplus and salvage, and frequently production planning and control." **(2)**

Certainly, such a restructuring consolidates functions and tends to avoid duplication of efforts. In addition, it places under one departmental head the responsibility for controlling and reducing materials costs which, as we have seen, can account for greater than 50% of total costs incurred in producing a product. Consequently, its implementation requires, indeed demands, teamwork and inter- departmental cooperation.

Materials Management, as a function and not an individual, has the decided advantage of managing from a company-wide perspective. In the real world, however, this advantage is attacked from every angle. The Materials Manager may coordinate the activities of both Purchasing and Production Planning, but that does not mean that the two departments won't tend to still see the world in a more narrow focus. Materials Management expands the focus, but its success depends on the same human elements which are the boon and bane of all company activities. That is why we stress cooperation and team-building. It is also why we advocate the introduction of the JIT/TQC philosophy of business. This total business concept reinforces the structure of Materials Management with the girders of a new mind-set.

Another restructuring is internal to Purchasing. It is the Buyer/Planner concept. This was driven home to us at a seminar we conducted. At lunch, we were talking to two women who were discussing how to interface buying with Material Requirement Planning (MRP). One woman said that her job was analysis, taking the MRP output and telling Purchasing what to buy. The other woman, the buyer, then did the buying from suppliers.

We then explained the concept of a Buyer/Planner to them. Why don't you restructure your jobs, we said, so that each of you has both a planning and procurement function. Divide the items which the MRP says you must procure and be responsible for both buying and planning the items for which you have authority. As you can see, this is similar to the Materials Management concept in that one person is accountable for material from the planning stage through the purchasing stage. The Buyer/Planner concept also structures a job description around function, rather than department and this, we feel, is highly desirable. It serves to make Purchasing part of the MRP base because now it is possible to go directly from MRP execution to the purchase order, or supplier via electronic data transfer. Lastly, the Buyer/Planner solidifies the relationship between internal company operations and suppliers. A buyer no longer has to get back to a planner when a supplier has a delivery or production question. That person is the planner as well as the buyer. The responsibility and authority for inventory, purchasing, planning and logistics falls to one person.

So far, we have discussed internal transitions. Now we turn our attention to external ones. Once again, since materials content accounts for such a large percentage of product cost, it makes sense to be concerned with supplier relations. JIT/TQC purchasing will not work unless frequent, small deliveries of "zero-defect" parts can be assured. What, then, should be the interface with suppliers? And, how should one go about selecting suppliers who can work with you in a JIT/TQC purchasing environment?

The cardinal rule in developing a supplier partnership will be a radical departure from accepted purchasing norms for some. It is the transformation of the relationship between you and your supplier into a partnership in which the same principles of communication and teamwork apply as do those internal to your company. It is nothing more, and nothing less, than the elevation of the supplier from victim to partner.

The suppliers know their business. If you don't trust your suppliers, then why are you dealing with them? Given that they know what they are doing, it is reasonable to seek their advice and tap their expertise. From now on, when you sit down with suppliers and give them a list of your needs, seek out and listen to their feedback. Make them understand that a partnership is not only essential to the demands of frequent, small, defect-free deliveries in a JIT/TQC relationship, but will benefit them as much as it does you. In effect, you are telling your suppliers that you will commit your company to a long-term relationship, if they are willing to commit their companies to the practices and philosophies of JIT/TQC.

You promise to share production schedules, forecasting and engineering information with them so they are able to construct their own schedules with reliability. In turn, suppliers allow you to evaluate their operations and processes and to monitor their performance. We will discuss these in more detail in Chapter 4 on Total Quality Control. How to develop this relationship will be covered in the next chapter. The present discussion is to point out the direction in which you will be heading and to give you some ideas on how to select suppliers who will be able to travel the same route.

Separating the wheat from the chaff, the good supplier from the bad, has been, and will always remain, an important duty of Purchasing. Indeed, in JIT/TQC purchasing, supplier selection may even gain in importance, since single and sole suppliers are not unheard of and are even desirable.

First, let's clearly define the terms of sole-, single-, and multiple-source supplier. A sole-source supplier is unique. This company provides a part which you need that no other company in the universe makes. A single-source supplier is a company you have chosen to be the supplier of the part for a number of reasons, hopefully ones which rely on cost-effectiveness and capacity requirements. With a single-source supplier, however, you have the option when demand increases to turn to other suppliers to meet your needs. In JIT/TQC purchasing, you could use multiple-source suppliers in an effort to get frequent, on-time deliveries of the part. For example, in order to obtain weekly deliveries, you may select four suppliers who deliver monthly and stagger their shipments so that you receive the parts every week.

The aim of JIT/TQC purchasing is not to favor one sourcing philosophy over another, but to be flexible in selecting sources. We have found that most companies need to reduce dramatically the number of suppliers they use. Single-sourcing through Supplier Certification is the most desirable way to achieve this reduction. Subsequently, it is no longer our role simply to get the best price and handle all the clerical work associated with buying. As part of a company-wide team, especially linked with planning, Purchasing must find suppliers willing and capable of meeting the demands of Total Quality Control and of putting in place and maintaining strict manufacturing process controls. If the world was a neat and tidy place, you would only need to go out shopping at various factories where you could inspect their "labels" and see who has what you want. But, sourcing requires looking beyond labels.

For example, one company you select may be a major supplier of one part. This company can also be a minor supplier (second source) of another part. Also, two sets of tooling at the same supplier equals a second source. Don't lock yourself into relationships with suppliers in which you cannot change. This is not to

your benefit or to your supplier's. In a relationship based on
flexibility, you and the supplier are able to take advantage of the
low inventory and reduced costs which come with JIT/TQC. But
to gain that advantage, both of you need to share information
which is the grease for the JIT/TQC wheels.

There are three areas of information to study when selecting
suppliers. They are:

1. Objective performance data.
2. Long-term vitality and financial responsibility.
3. Technical leadership and know-how.

The Buyer/Planners then look at the supplier base and with
these areas in mind ask the following questions about each
supplier:

1. Where are the suppliers located?
2. How many items does each supply?
3. What is their quality capability?
4. What is the supplier's delivery performance?
5. What are their min/max capacity limits?
6. How responsive is the supplier to change?

We have discussed supplier selection here with a caveat in
mind. It is impossible to cut this activity away from the whole
without losing some important connections. For example, the first
area above ties directly to supplier certification and the role played
by both Quality Control and Purchasing in achieving TQC. The
second area involves communication between Finance and Purchasing in establishing long-term contracts and relationships with
suppliers in good financial health. The last area connects Engineering and Manufacturing with Purchasing by creating an atmosphere where technological expertise can be shared and tapped by
both your company and the supplier. To paraphrase the old axiom,
"*information is money*", a lot of money.

Thus, we warn you not to venture into supplier selection
without reading further so that you can understand the complex

network, the spider's web, which connects the different parts of JIT/TQC. But, to give you some idea of how sourcing philosophy and supplier selection works, we introduce the concept of systems contracting.

Systems contracting is a pre-negotiated contract for goods from a single source. It is a long-term contract (e.g., 5 years with a 30-day cancellation for non-performance) which employs direct requisitioning (the user releases directly with the supplier bypassing purchasing, stores, etc.). The rationale behind this system is that the effective management of money does not require Purchasing to handle repetitive purchase orders. Purchasing, however, does have the responsibility for supplier performance in much the same way that Finance has the responsibility for overall budgeting, but not the day-to-day budgeting of each department. Also, remember that systems contracting is not the same as a blanket order which is annually requoted and issued, comes with fixed quantities and prices, and where all requisitions go through Purchasing.

And, since requisitions don't go through Purchasing, your first step in implementing systems contracting is to design a system which will handle basically the signalling of orders and receipts. This can be handled manually, beginning with the initial contract and paperwork and with a minimum of documentation, but it is clear that systems contracting lends itself to what has been called "paperless purchasing."

"Paperless purchasing" uses computers, even personal computers, to form a network of Electronic Data Interchange (EDI). Bar coding is also often used. The idea is to work with a common data base (between you and the supplier and between departments in your company) which automatically records requisitions and receipt of orders while simultaneously updating the status of your contract with the supplier. These activities occur both in your company's EDI system and in your supplier's.

A recent column in *The New York Times* identifies the advantages of EDI as "savings in time and money, reductions in lead times, inventory and carrying costs, improvement of cash flow." It goes on to note that both the trucking and grocery industry are "struggling doggedly toward electronic data interchange" in order "to emulate the just-in-time inventory approach to manufacturing championed by the Japanese." **(3)** Although a single, common standard of interchange is not quite a reality, the benefits of "paperless purchasing" are great enough that these industries are moving ahead. Indeed, part of your negotiating in systems contracting may center around the adoption of a standard between you and your suppliers.

Once the system and standard is in place, one accurate and convenient method of effecting the interchange is with the use of bar coding. Walter Merrill, Materials Manager at the Computervision plant in New Hampshire, has done this. To walk into his company's receiving area and watch the movement of material from the door to the line is a truly surprising experience. Where's all the paperwork? Where's all those pink and yellow and green slips? It's too clean in here! We will discuss how Computervision achieved their version of "paperless purchasing" in more detail in a case study appearing in Chapter 11.

Getting back on the track of implementation, you can apply systems contracting to Maintenance, Repair and Operating (MRO) supplies, raw material and proprietary items. But, we recommend that you do not start with a major commodity. Even though systems contracting applies to all phases of JIT/TQC purchasing, start simple and build on your achievements. After you have chosen the items with which to start, determine the cost savings and sell top management on the idea of systems contracting. Since this new method will circumvent old rules and makes the route between supplier and user much more direct, you will find some Purchasing activities either eliminated or reduced. Obviously, these are the points you wish to bring up with top management. The following lists show you what will be eliminated and reduced:

ELIMINATIONS

Purchase orders	Acknowledgements
Expediting	Back orders
Inventory	Sales calls to Purchasing
More than one invoice per month	

REDUCTIONS

Costs   Paperwork
Cost of inventory   Workload in Purchasing
Phone calls to suppliers   Emergencies
Delays between requisitioner,
Purchasing and supplier

Let's take an easy example. Every month, you buy 2 cases of paper clips in 10 boxes of 1,000. You do this every month, every year without fail. You know some paper clips turn into ear-cleaners, some get sucked up by vacuum cleaners, etc. but 20,000 clips a month serves your purpose. Currently, you send a purchase order every month to your stationery supplier asking for 2 cases. He sends back an acknowledgement; the cases come with an invoice which goes from receiving to Purchasing; the cases are placed in a closet and doled out by a grizzly inventory clerk who wants to know the whereabouts of every clip you have used and why you are so wasteful. Now, every month, your own Purchasing department gets a case (Purchasing uses a lot of paper clips!). Your office manager then locks that case in another closet. Finally, your secretary gets a box of 1,000 which she locks in her desk drawer. When you want a paper clip, you have to beg, borrow or steal.

Systems contracting can eliminate this humiliation and inefficiency. You know how many clips you will need over the next year (or more even). So, you tell your stationer, "Sue, this year I'm going to buy 240,000 paper clips. But, I want to make a new arrangement with you. I'm sick and tired of going through all the paperwork involved in requisitioning two cases a month. I'll bet you are, too. I know you will always have paper clips in stock. So, from now on, let's have a contract which says I will buy 240,000 paper clips at an agreed upon price and you will deliver them to my company as the storeroom releases them, based on actual requests.

But no supplier, you say, is going to throw a box of 1,000 paper clips on a truck because somebody in your Engineering department ran out of paper clips. Perhaps not. However, it is extremely likely that you do not buy only paper clips from Sue, the stationer.

It is also likely that you will be systems contracting for a number of office supplies and, in that case, it is to Sue's benefit and profit to go along with you. But, aren't we just pushing inventory off on the supplier? Not necessarily. As part of your implementation of a systems contract, you have gone through old invoices and determined a usage history for each item. You share this history with your supplier so that she knows what to expect from your company and, thus, can order appropriately for her own warehouse. This, as you can see, takes coordination and communication. It means that if you see a blip in paper clip consumption appearing in the future, you have to alert her.

And it works. Having worked at Digital Equipment Corporation and Allied Signal, we established a relationship with suppliers in which supplies were delivered to each department's secretary as that person placed releases against the contract. Not only did the supplier deliver in small quantities and on time, but to each individual location or secretary. Variations of this also exist where the supplier will consign material to your site and charge you based on consumption.

The elimination and reduction of certain purchasing activities will place more pressure on your department to perform better in the next stage of implementing systems contracting. That stage is supplier selection, of which we have talked about before. Here are some more detailed steps.

Supplier Selection

The first step is evaluation of the supplier base and the transition from old methods to the new criteria:

1. Look for new systems — suppliers with state-of-the-art material and processes.
2. Look for aggressiveness and progressiveness — suppliers with adaptability, flexibility and the ability to work with you.
3. Proximity to your location — a relative criteria; suppliers with JIT delivery are "close" no matter where they are located.

4. _Delivery performanc_e — suppliers who can deliver zero-defect parts accurately, frequently, on time and just-in-time.

5. _Breadth and depth of management_ — suppliers whose management is committed to working in a win/win environment.

6. _Performance of Inventory_ — suppliers whose management of their own inventory reflects JIT/TQC principles.

Considering the above criteria, you rate each potential or existing supplier as follows:

EXCELLENT	9-10
GOOD	7-8
FAIR	5-6
POOR	3-4
CORRECTABLE	1-2
UNSATISFACTORY	0

The rating chart looks something like the Michelin guide to restaurants or a critic's guide to movies. The analogy is not so far-fetched because of one very important, but often overlooked, point. Restaurant reviewers and movie critics eat dinners and watch films before they make their judgements. Facts and figures may look neat and tidy, but when you visit a supplier and see a chaotic shipping department, you have to wonder whether that supplier can do what it claims.

And go one step farther than the critics and reviewers. Bring along a somebody acquainted with how the product is processed in your plant to assist you with your evaluation. If you have adopted the team approach to purchasing, you would have probably done this automatically. Such a person has a far better understanding of the part than you will ever have. He works with the part. He knows that a burr which creates no problems for the supplier will need to be filed down before your machines can use the part. Maybe you are getting a great price (better than the supplier down the street), but what is the cost of cleaning up the part in terms of time and money. Your expert will be able to give you an idea.

Naturally, the supplier with the most points wins. That company will be most open to systems contracting and JIT/TQC purchasing. One last point needs to be made in selecting the supplier: Select first, then negotiate. In JIT/TQC purchasing, some points, like quality, are not negotiable. But before we discuss negotiation and purchasing agreements, let's look at an example of source selection as practiced in the real world.

Interviewed in an article appearing in *Purchasing*, Katherine M. Danforth, supervisor of purchasing at Sandia National Laboratories, Albuquerque, says she uses a formula in her systems contracting which measures the following:

> Financial status
> Product quality
> Physical layout
> Administrative talent
> Engineering talent
> Service **(4)**

She then uses this information to evaluate the suppliers in three weighted categories:

1. Supplier's ability to meet service level   — 45 pts
2. Management skills   — 15 pts
3. Competitive pricing   — 40 pts **(5)**

Negotiation

As we have said, price isn't everything. Cost plays a major role as well and, in negotiation, both must be balanced.

Negotiation in JIT/TQC purchasing rests on the two premises we introduced in Chapter 1: the total cost concept and the creation of a partnership with suppliers. You should use the evaluation techniques above in selecting potential suppliers with these two premises in mind. The number of points you award is directly linked to whether you believe this supplier can provide the lowest cost and can join with you in a mutually beneficial partnership. Doing so can be likened to finding a job. The best way is to narrow down the field of potential employers until you find one which needs you as much as you need them. These intangibles are sometimes overlooked as often as qualities like progressiveness and aggressiveness, management skills, and engineering talent at the supplier's plant. You could almost ask yourself if you would like to work at your supplier's company. If you answer "yes," it probably indicates that they are either employing concepts similar to yours or are willing to do so.

In a sense, what we have described above is the mind-set you must adopt before beginning negotiation. It is identical to the JIT/TQC mind-set, that is, the whole is mirrored in the part. Thus, you should keep in mind the following three axioms when negotiating:

1. Quality is not a negotiated item. The terms for quality are the acceptance of a zero-defect program at the supplier's plant.
2. Terms and conditions should be negotiated only once — the first time you negotiate the agreement.
3. Purchasing will now be required to obtain long-term agreements for the life of the product.

Information is the most powerful negotiating tool ever devised. With information from a number of your own departments, you are in a far better position to convince a supplier of the necessity of your demands. Buyer/planners and users, as we have noted, are more adept at answering questions which pertain to lead times, scheduling and production, forecasts, inventory control. At the least, you will appear to have done your homework when you sit down with a supplier to negotiate. But, more importantly, you have entered negotiations as a model of what you want your supplier to be like. You are giving this company the opportunity to participate in a profitable partnership. And that is a powerful negotiating tool.

Another important area of negotiation focuses on supplier

performance. Chapter 4 addresses the specifics of supplier certification, that is, the control and management of supplier performance as it relates to total quality control. But, supplier performance also covers areas like on-time delivery, error and waste elimination, and any of the other facets of JIT/TQC philosophy. In short, you constantly monitor each of your supplier's performances and measure them. This serves not only to alert you to errors or missed delivery dates, but acts as a statistical process control (SPC). It is enough for you to know at this point that a documented process control at a supplier's plant can predict and manage problems. Then, you and the supplier can work to eliminate the underlying causes. In other words, you gain visibility. Once more, we see how far the web spun by JIT/TQC extends.

Purchasing Agreement

The result of negotiation is a purchasing agreement which incorporates the principles described above (from which you should never waver) and the means to achieve those principles. The basic differences between a "normal" purchasing agreement and one in a JIT/TQC environment have to do mostly with monitoring performance or supplier certification. To sum up, the key points in a JIT/TQC purchasing agreement should include provisions for:

1. Quality — zero defects
2. Quantities — flexibility
3. Long-term agreements
4. Lead-time reduction
5. Performance — a commitment to control manufacturing operations to insure TQC
6. JIT/on-time delivery

In a word, commitment. Both you and the supplier have committed yourselves to a long-term relationship where the supplier is a partner, not a victim.

A final word here about ethics. In JIT/TQC purchasing, long-term partnerships and sole- or single-source suppliers rule as well as the emphasis on cost over price. Therefore, Purchasing is not concerned as much with ethical behavior when soliciting bids. Fairness does come into play, however, in the selection stage. Certainly, each potential supplier should be allowed the same opportunities and information and should be alerted to the way in which you will evaluate. Not surprisingly, JIT/TQC purchasing makes ethics a practical issue. Since timely delivery of quality parts is so essential to the workings of JIT/TQC, we must not choose a supplier for any other reason than their ability to perform. Favoritism is simply bad business in a situation where you rely on a strong partnership with your supplier which is based on mutual trust.

Fortunately, the vast majority of people reading this book are totally ethical in their dealings with suppliers. The basic tenets of the purchasing profession require that we not only remain ethical, but also have every appearance of absolute ethical behavior. The same holds true in the JIT/TQC arena. The National Association of Purchasing Management (NAPM) has established ethical guidelines for the profession. These are guidelines which should be reviewed from time to time for what they can tell us about trust and ethics. A basic premise is that if you think it is wrong, it probably is.

CHAPTER THREE: From Supplier to Production Line

So far, we have placed an emphasis on relationships, networks, and webs when discussing JIT/TQC purchasing. Now the time has come to divide JIT/TQC and explore individually the relationships contained in each of its parts. In this chapter, we will examine the portion of JIT which involves Purchasing. You will see that it means more than on-time delivery as the popular phrase, "just-in-time delivery," would lead you to believe. Our more inclusive meaning has everything to do with material management and procurement — from supplier relationships to inventory management to production scheduling to shipping on time to your customers.

Let's start by debunking two myths. The first myth states that JIT is a method for dumping inventory on suppliers, requiring them to hold stock you would normally store in your own storerooms and warehouses. There's an easy answer to this. If your suppliers run their businesses according to the philosophy of JIT, then they only stock the material used to produce orders as needed. The supplier gets stock delivered just-in-time. Does that mean we merely dump inventory on suppliers? Somebody, somewhere, is left holding the goods and that person will pass on inventory carrying costs in the form of higher prices. There's no free ride, not even with JIT.

But, when Henry Ford first began building cars, he employed a JIT system so efficient that it took less than four days to produce his product — four days, that is, from mining iron ore to finished car. Sure, you object, but nobody these days has the vertical integration that Henry Ford enjoyed. We agree. The real world is not as rosy as our easy answer indicates. Ford proved, however, that it is possible. Keep in mind that in earlier days, changeovers were far and few between. Current auto practice is to shut down for a length of time between model changeovers, a far cry from Ford's original objectives.

How, then, can we achieve what Ford did in a more difficult world today? How can we employ JIT without dumping inventory on our suppliers? First of all, it would not make much economic sense for us to dump inventory. Eventually, we will pay for it in higher prices charged by our suppliers. What we need to do is teach our suppliers to employ JIT as well, to travel the road together, to make slow and steady progress. Nowhere in this book will we claim that JIT/TQC can be achieved in one gulp. You will be cautioned to start in one area where results will be highly visible and then to spread the gospel. For suppliers, you begin JIT with one product or class of products. When the supplier and you both feel this is working, then you add more products. You never dump inventory if you are truly employing JIT, simply because your suppliers are moving in the same direction with you. And if they aren't willing, select another supplier. And if you are stuck with a supplier who won't budge, employ JIT elsewhere, with other suppliers, with other material. But don't ever stop attempting to convince your suppliers to adopt JIT and TQC.

The second myth states that JIT is an inventory reduction plan. That is a consequence of JIT and is not broad enough to define the totality of the business philosophy. As an example, let's take Kanban, the tool Toyota uses in Japan to achieve JIT. Kanban is a system whereby cards are shuttled back and forth between work stations to control the amount of inventory and production. Imagine two work stations, A and B. A works on parts assembled by B. A receives an order (probably a Kanban card from the station ahead of it). A sends a card to B asking for one part. B finds the card in its bin and assembles the part so that it may send it along to A. To assemble the part, B sends a card to the work station or stations behind it. Kanban, then, is a chain whereby only what needs to be built is indeed actually built. Nothing is stored in finished goods warehouses.

Now, let's say when a company begins a Kanban program, it uses 10 cards representing the number of production units. As we mentioned above, companies should not start at the end of the process. In other words, move gradually toward your goal. In doing so, you will find that Kanban also acts as a production control technique. Everything moves smoothly, but there is still excess in the system. What should you do? Reduce the number of cards. Now, reducing can present problems such as bottlenecks, inventory shortages or long set-up times. You must view that as an opportunity. JIT, above all, gives you visibility into the workings of your production line.

Think back to the cartoon with the monsters in Chapter 1. JIT allows you to chart a course which not only maneuvers you through the troubled waters, but helps you eliminate the problems like a dredger which opens up shipping channels in busy harbors. In Japan, they are so zealous about dredging up and eliminating problems that they will stop production lines to fix problems. Unlike many of us, they don't throw more inventory into the lake, and thus raise the inventory level.

JIT has an impact on every department associated with production. Where does Purchasing fit into this scheme? We believe Purchasing's first priority is to develop new directions with suppliers and to become involved with the supplier's plant and processes. All the internal adjusting in the world will not work without the just-in-time delivery of zero-defect parts. We have already pointed out in the previous chapters the need to establish long-term partnerships with suppliers, to select suppliers based on their ability to employ JIT/TQC, and to monitor and measure their adherence to performance standards. Perhaps the most important direction, however, is to view JIT and TQC as problem-solving techniques rather than merely an inventory reduction plan or a means to dump inventory or a production control tool. To do so is to miss the forest for the trees.

We have already discussed the philosophy behind JIT or stockless production. You can think of the emphasis on problem-solving as the forest, or context, in which you will implement JIT activities. This requires examining the trees which surround you. At first, you may think you have left the purchasing forest, but we will shortly show you how all the paths connect.

We all deal with costs. There are fixed costs such as set-ups and acquisitions. There are variable costs such as labor, material and burden. Together, they make up the total cost of a product. For example, suppose the set-up cost for a product is $10.00 and the material, labor and burden costs are $1.00. Then the cost of making one product is $11.00; the cost of making two parts is $6.00 each. This is because we can amortize the set-up cost of $10.00 over the number of products we produce. Therefore, the higher the lot size, the more bang we get for each set-up dollar. Ten products for example would bring the set-up cost down to $1.00 for each product.

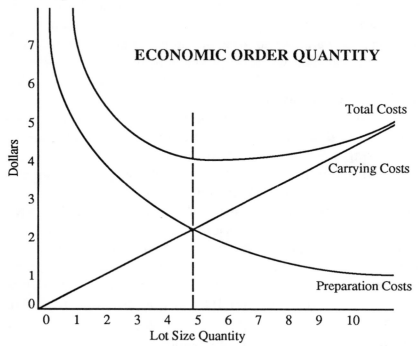

It comes as no surprise then that manufacturers have wanted to produce as many products as possible for each given set-up. Large lot sizes seem to drive costs down. But, look at the graph. Carrying costs are an offsetting factor. It costs money to keep enough material around to produce large lot sizes. If inventory was free, we would buy as much as we could or make as much as we could. Given this constraint, manufacturers have used an Economic Order Quantity (EOQ) formula to determine the lowest total cost and then have procured material in accordance with its dictates.

Sounds good and logical, doesn't it? But there are problems with EOQ. First of all, it is a deterministic model. It assumes that you know what the demand for your product will be. Past history and current orders may point to a demand of 400 pieces, but you are tempted to make the lot size 500 because that will drive your costs down further and you are sure Sales can sell the rest. But, by doing this you are proving that you don't live in a deterministic world. Indeed, it is a probablistic world where future demand is not known beyond a shadow of doubt. Nobody, however, likes to live in such an "iffy" world. Even Albert Einstein tried to prove that God doesn't roll dice. So you pretend you can push all 500 pieces through the line and hope that your customers will buy. Your hope and your allegiance to EOQ is so strong that you overlook the carrying costs of large piles of work-in-process and finished goods inventory. To Finance people, those are normal operating costs. However, the objective is to employ the total cost concept.

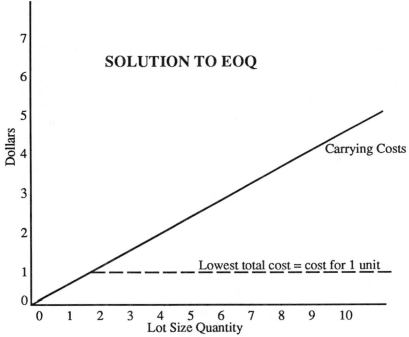

You look at set-up and acquisition costs in the same manner. There's nothing I can do about them, you say. Wrong, we say. This is where JIT enters the picture. You can reduce, even eliminate, set-up and acquisition costs through a three-part program:

1. Begin a supplier lead-time reduction program.
2. Use systems contracts (certainly for A parts, or the 20% which account for 80% of the cost).
3. Develop a partnership environment with suppliers.

What does our costs graph look like now? Now that we have eliminated some variables. In reality, of course, you will not completely eliminate them, but the purpose of the graph on the preceeding page is to show where you would end. In mathematical terms, you can liken this process of elimination to that of a series approaching its limit. It never quite touches, but it can get so close that one doesn't care about the miniscule difference. So, too, should you reorient yourselves. The graph below shows the limit. You work to approach it.

As you can see, the lowest total cost equals the cost of making one unit. When set-up and acquisition costs are eliminated, the greatest drag on profit is high carrying costs. EOQ assumes you can't change set-up and acquisition costs. The importance of carrying costs, therefore, gets buried under the need to carry more inventory to get that all-important break on set-up amortization. Today, this reasoning doesn't make sense for two reasons:

1. JIT set-up reduction programs dramatically reduce lot sizes.
2. Inventory carrying costs are becoming increasingly expensive (2-3% per month). Some of these costs are:

> Cost of Money
> Depreciation and Obsolescence
> Material Handling
> Warehousing (Total)
> Insurance and Taxes
> Opportunity Costs

Let's say that it takes one hour to set up a machine and it costs $10.00. JIT says (and it has been repeatedly proven around this country and in the Far East) you can reduce the set-up time. That's one-twentieth of the time and roughly one-twentieth of the cost, or 50 cents instead of $10.00. Where, now, is the great advantage of producing lot sizes of 500. In fact, holding that much inventory will drive your carrying costs so high that they will substantially eat away at profit. It will be cheaper, then, to build only in a lot size of one with JIT. We also pay a set-up person for eight hours work a day. Then why are we worried about how many set-ups are done each day?

Today's JIT means you buy or make only the number of units you need which is determined by actual customer demand. The customer pulls the products through your line (while you pull from your supplier). You don't push them into warehouses. So, your goal is to produce one lot at a time and to constantly reduce the lot size until you reach one part.

SUPPLIER   MANUFACTURER   CUSTOMER

You also establish a program to eliminate set-up costs at your plant as well as at the suppliers' plants.

You realize and abide by the rule that the smaller the lot size, the smaller the storage inventory and the smaller the carrying costs.

You consider each area in your plant as a station of assembly and that includes your suppliers as an extension of the plant.

What we are talking about is the Theory of One which says:

> Operators on a line obtain only as much material as they need to make one product. This is accomplished by planning for less material and by minimizing queues so that we only provide that material which a work station can produce in its cycle time. (1)

You may have noticed we have been using the words push and pull. This was to emphasize that JIT works best with a pull system of manufacturing in which the Theory of One provides the foundation. A pull system is like the Kanban system we described earlier. Final assembly gets a request for a product in the form of a customer order. It turns back to subassembly lines and pulls parts to make the finished product. Those subassembly lines are composed of work stations which pull from other work stations or suppliers behind them and so on. Purchasing is required to supply the components needed by the work stations. And not only supply them, but supply them just-in-time and certified as zero defects. JIT, from Purchasing's view, is material flow through an integrated production process with minimal lead-times and no excess inventory.

JIT's external components depend on the integration of on-time delivery, supplier certification and quality. On-time delivery tightens the supply chain so there are shorter lead times. Often, at this point, critics contend that the greater distances in America make JIT delivery impossible. Distance is no deterrent. Certify your suppliers and they will understand that timely delivery is a major factor in whether they become or remain suppliers. In turn, assure them that you will communicate daily the changes in your forecast and production schedule based on actual, real-time sales. Our intent is to avoid stockpiles of inventory in anticipation of demand changes.

You can make this promise when the internal components of JIT are in place. As we have said, you must reduce lot sizes and set-up times so that you are in a position to manage the flow of material, not inventory. It has been estimated that as little as 5% of the time you hold inventory results in real work being performed on the material, that is, work which transforms the material into a saleable product. That means 95% of the time you are paying for something that does nothing.

To manage the flow of material effectively relies heavily upon whether you know what your present status is. It reminds us of the two explorers who struggle up a mountain for days. When they get to the top, one explorer turns to the other and says, "Where are we?" His friend pores over the map, checks his compass, looks at the sun and finally speaks. "See that mountain over there," he says as he points across a valley. "We're on top of it."

Accuracy

Inventory accuracy is vital to JIT. Your relationships with suppliers depends upon it. Otherwise, you might end up telling them you are on the wrong mountain top. You must know which mountain you are sitting on. Inventory accuracy with respect to purchasing records and supplier inventory control is the first requirement of JIT.

How do you reach the accuracy levels required by JIT? First, let's digress for a moment and mention what we call the "98% or 99% Syndrome." Most people, if you asked them, would be satisfied to be right 98% or 99% of the time. If their record accuracy was at that level, they would be content (some would even be ecstatic). Suppose, however, that you asked them how they would feel if their pay checks and bank statements were going to be accurate 98 or 99% of the time. Maybe, their pay check is $500 a week, but once every two years or so, Payroll is going to make a mistake and only give them $50.00 a week. Do you think they will accept that? Of course not, but they did say before that they would accept a 98% or 99% level of accuracy.

The point is that there are many places in our lives where we accept nothing less than 100% as the following shows:

WHAT YOU'D GET FROM "99.9% SUPPLIERS"

- At least 20,000 wrong drug prescriptions each year.
- More than 15,000 newborn babies accidentally dropped by doctors/nurses each year.
- Two short or long landings at O'Hare airport each day (Also New York, Los Angeles, Atlanta, etc.).
- Nearly 500 incorrect surgical operations per week.

We are saying that record and inventory accuracy should not be excluded from this goal:

100% ACCURACY 100% OF THE TIME.

You certainly are not going to reach that level in one big step. Again, you are going to abide by the Rule of Halves which states that you move half the way to your goal. When you reach that point, you set your next goal. And you keep doing this until you reach 100%.

We advocate that you adopt the attitude that it can be done. Next, you gradually work toward bringing all the data, information and material records in your company up to the 100% level. Perhaps most importantly, you now monitor accuracy to detect variations which deviate beyond accepted levels. A method we advocate here is cycle counting, that is, cycle counting in which you do not simply count and then change figures, but count and audit your figures. When there is a deviation, you immediately set out to find the source of the problem. You don't live with it. You don't cover it with safety stock. You eliminate the problem causing the deviation, because if you don't, you can be sure the problem will pop up again. As a rule of thumb, we recommend that you count "A" items 6 times a year and "C" items 1 time. Eliminate "B" items.

While we are on counting, one easy way to improve accuracy is to use standard containers. The classic example is an egg carton. Who counts the number of eggs in a carton when they go to the store? Nobody. There are 12 slots and if they are all filled, then there are 12 eggs. As you can see, there is no chance of counting wrong simply because there is no counting, but just matching slots to items. The same principle is readily applicable to the manufacturing environment. Suppliers deliver in standard containers, the size determined by the requirements of the production line to which the parts will be delivered.

Bar Coding Applications and JIT

C.J. (Chip) Long, Senior Vice President of Professionals for Technology Associates, Inc., found bar coding to be an excellent aid in achieving accuracy, although not as inexpensive as standard containers. However, bar coding does have benefits beyond accuracy, timeliness of reporting and tracking. Those other benefits have to do with making this data base accessible to all departments of a company. That type of network can lay the foundation for new technologies. Ideally, of course, you would connect your data base and bar coding system through an Electronic Data Interchange (EDI) with the supplier. Then, there would not even be a need to send paperwork or purchase orders. The supplier would be alerted through the EDI system; even bills could be paid in this manner. Faster payment of bills can ease the transition by suppliers to the frequent, small deliveries demanded by JIT.

Although Computervision, a CAD/CAM manufacturer and client located in Manchester, New Hampshire, does not have all these new technologies in place, it has made significant progress as a pioneer in the use of bar coding. Walter Merrill, Manager of Materials Control, describes bar coding as the "ultimate link between humans, materials, and machines." (2) Another, more recent, article describes the extent of their progress in this way:

> "[The kit picking system] is only a portion of the wholly integrated bar coded manufacturing system used by Computervision. The company has bar coded labels for inter-plant material transfers, for identifying tested integrated

circuits on their computer boards, for receiving and tracking systems or parts of systems returned for repairs, for inventory taking, for testing and tracking printed circuit boards in production, and for tracking capital assets. In the stockrooms, more than ten employees daily use the bar code system; throughout the plant, more than 100 use it each day." **(3)**

Clearly, they have come a long way. Merrill points out that the biggest obstacle may well be acceptance by suppliers. He maintains that the best way to begin implementation is "to educate them to your bar coding objectives, and have them apply bar code labels where indicated by visual aids supplied by you." **(4)** Furthermore, he says that the transition can be made easier by actually supplying the labels to your suppliers.

What is the result of such a sophisticated system of bar coding? Merrill reports that "the speed attained in reading bar code with 99% accuracy is 4-5 times faster than data entry via normal keypunching." **(5)**

From Ship-To-Stock
to Ship-To-WIP (Work-In-Process)

Now that we have traveled some paths through the JIT forest and looked at the trees, it is time to take an overall look. For us, the point of JIT delivery, production, inventory is to adjust from the philosophy of "ship-to-stock" to the philosophy of "ship-to-WIP." Let's pretend the supplier's truck is outside our door. What do we do now?

First of all, you may wonder just how it got to your door. Whose responsibility is that? In a JIT environment, transportation may fall under the umbrella of Purchasing. First, delivery schedules are now part of the negotiations which lead to an agreement. If a supplier can't guarantee delivery performance, no agreement. Second, transportation is vital to the operation of your plant. You don't store safety stock inventories any more. What happens if a delivery is late? The production line stops. That's not good. JIT is like a chain, only as strong as its weakest link. Third, transportation depends upon good relations with suppliers and transportation companies. These relations are supported by buyer/planners who know your company's material requirements and production schedules so they are able to guarantee stable procurement schedules with suppliers. They also have the responsibility and authority to structure, enforce and maintain delivery performance.

What we found in discussing the transportation systems in the Far East was a quote: "We think that big trucks equal big storerooms." What their objective is in utilizing small trucks is to only receive what they need in small quantities.

That truck we mentioned above is still outside your door. What are you going to do to get its contents directly to the line now that you have a transportation schedule which delivered on time?

Store the boxes and crates in Shipping and Receiving until a work station needs them? That's not JIT.

Tell the truck to wait until a work station requests the parts? That's not JIT and that certainly won't please your supplier who is paying for the truck's time or your Finance department if your company is paying.

Put the parts in a warehouse with its own receiving department and when we need them over here at the production facility, we will call up and tell them to ship to us? That certainly isn't JIT. Many companies are doing this, but it doesn't solve anything. You still have a truck outside, except now it's yours, not the supplier's.

Perhaps send the parts directly from Shipping and Receiving to the work station on the production line where they will be used? Now we are on to something.

This means shipping them to work-in-process. "Ship-to-WIP" is the movement of zero-defect material directly to the work station on the production line where it is needed, at just the time it is needed, in the quantity it is needed.

If this sounds similar to the Theory of One, there is a reason. They are two sides of the same coin. They both rely on a pull system of manufacturing. When a work station needs a part, it is delivered to the station precisely at the moment it is requested, whether the source is another work station or an outside supplier. Perhaps the key to "ship-to-WIP" is to think of outside suppliers as one more work station in a production line. The only differences are that they are not at the manufacturing site and you don't own them.

We say "only differences" with a smile of recognition. They may be the only differences, but they are big differences. How do you get a supplier to act like one of your own work stations? The answer, of course, is dependent on Purchasing's role in developing good supplier relationships, in making the supplier part of the team.

In establishing a "ship-to-WIP" program, you cover much of the same ground as in supplier selection. Here are seven guidelines for you to follow:

1. Evaluate supplier's ability to provide total quality control and delivery performance.
2. Present advantages of JIT delivery and TQC product to supplier's management.

3. Conduct a complete and detailed quality survey of supplier.
4. Draft a plan incorporating total quality control and on-time delivery performance and the responsibilities of both customer and supplier.
5. Review and modify the plan with suppliers and listen carefully to their suggestions.
6. Establish a supplier quality engineer to act as a contact between you and the supplier.
7. Put the plan into action. Audit and maintain it through random sampling and Statistical Process Control/ Statistical Quality Control (SPC/SQC).

You probably noticed that when you work on supplier relations in this "ship-to-WIP" program, you do not only work on JIT problems. Quality is inseparable from JIT when you ship to work-in-process. The reason is quite simple: Since there are no safety stocks to turn to when bad parts arrive, there is no other choice than to shut down the line. Obviously, you don't want to do this and you won't have to. That is, if Purchasing, as part of the JIT team, has also established a Total Quality Control (TQC) program, the subject of the next chapter.

CHAPTER FOUR: Supplier Partnerships: The Certification Process

To achieve a successful JIT Purchasing program, we must adopt a Total Quality Control (TQC) approach. This approach divides into two main thrusts. The first is a shifting of emphasis from a storeroom mentality to the mentality of shipping directly to the manufacturing line. This thrust avoids extra counting and control requirements such as Incoming Inspection.

The second thrust is to require suppliers to improve the quality of their products and, thus, to deliver zero-defect components to our production lines. We strive toward this goal in a partnership with our suppliers via a Supplier Certification program. This may seem demanding, especially for smaller companies, but we will see in this chapter that the four pillars of certification are not overly difficult and have benefits for all parties:

Consistent measurements
Conformance to requirements
On-time delivery
Process Controls

Quality is not a nebulous term. At least it shouldn't be. It is a measurable and thus controllable entity. Many think of it as some sort of beautiful, unattainable cumulus cloud that floats on the breeze's whim across a deep, blue sky. Zero-defects, or TQC, is beautiful, but that does not mean we should lie down and daydream about how wonderful it would be if we could have this dream come true in our factories. The Far East certainly has not laid down.

In Japan, they have a rule called the "40/30/30 rule" which identifies the three major reasons for poor quality. The rule quite simply states that poor design accounts for 40% of quality problems, errors in the manufacturing process account for 30%, and defective parts from suppliers account for the last 30%. In this chapter, we will concentrate on the second and third percentage areas and treat the first 40% when we discuss the TQC/Engineering interface.

Quality, from Purchasing's perspective, mainly centers around the relationships with suppliers. We will focus on the role played by Purchasing to insure delivery of zero-defect products to the manufacturing line so that Production can do its best work. There are both technical and developmental parts to this process. The two areas we will discuss are:

> Supplier Certification
> Statistical Process Control (SPC).

The theme of quality means: *MAKE IT RIGHT THE FIRST TIME*. This places an emphasis on defect prevention so that routine inspection is no longer needed. Consequently, the burden of proof will not rest upon Inspectors, but on the makers of a part, whether they be machinists, foremen, or suppliers. These approaches will not work until management goes beyond paying lip-service to quality. After all, who is against quality? Management must know what TQC is and what they must do to achieve it. Responsibility is everywhere. Lastly, quality can not be inspected into a part; it must already be there.

If this sounds familiar, it is because these assertions are similar to those we used when talking about the new mind-set Purchasing must adopt. Not only are JIT and TQC interdependent, but they both require new ways of thinking:

> Prevention vs. Appraisal
> Quality Measurement vs. Hope that "IT" will happen
> Process Understanding vs. Product Incoming Inspection

Supplier relations are essential to a successful TQC program and developing those relations is the responsibility of Purchasing. What does supplier development mean? Do we become, in effect, their parents and scold them when they do wrong and praise them when they do right? Of course not! No supplier in this country will put up with that treatment and will use every opportunity to subvert the relationship.

When we say that you should make the supplier a part of your organization for the life of the product and the life of the company, we have specific ideas in mind, not a parental relationship. These ideas are based on the principle that as quality goes up, the price will inevitably be lower. And that is good for you and the supplier.

What are these specific ideas? We have touched on some already such as long-term contracts, advanced planning information, standardization, and EDI or interactive information systems. We have also discussed the need for frequent deliveries, coordinated freight schedules and the myth that geography is an obstacle when, in fact, careful planning can achieve all of these goals. What is left are goals and expectations covering supplier training and education in all aspects of quality improvement. This is achieved by teaching suppliers the concepts behind JIT and TQC.

To get to the teaching of supplier certification, however, requires two intermediate steps. The first is a complete understanding of quality goals and expectations. The second is a rating system which allows you to separate the wheat from the chaff so that you don't waste time on suppliers who will never be able to adapt to JIT/TQC purchasing.

Let's look at the goals and expectations first. As a goal, you want suppliers who claim quality ownership; who believe in the zero-defect concept ; and who maintain the capability to consistently meet the requirements for quality, quantity, cost, and delivery. Here is what you should expect from them:

SUPPLIER QUALITY EXPECTATIONS

1. Quality — conformance to your requirements at all times
2. Delivery — meeting your scheduled requirements
3. Quantity — providing the quantity ordered; no more, no less
4. Cost — reasonable profit margin and low total cost

In addition, you should expect to find the following standards in the supplier's quality process:

QUALITY PROCESS EXPECTATIONS

Supplier quality process should:

1. Create an improvement environment
2. Develop capability to measure quality improvement
3. Have short-term goal-setting capability to achieve zero-defect standards
4. Have long-term goal-setting capabilities to continue zero-defect standards
5. Be prevention-oriented rather than approval-oriented

Supplier Development

If this looks one-sided, remember what we mentioned earlier when we talked about negotiation. Quality, we said, is not a negotiated item. The terms and conditions for the delivery of zero-defect products are placed in a contract as a given. If you can conform to these requirements, it says, then we can do business. This does not mean that a supplier must achieve your standards in one big shot. The contract clearly states how quality improvement will proceed and how it will be monitored. The following gives you an idea of how the contract language should read:

CONTRACT QUALITY CLAUSE

Supplier accepts zero-defects as a quality standard and does not subscribe to the philosophy of acceptable levels of defective materials (AQL's). We will require information (quality evidence) on incoming defective rates with improvement benchmarks set for review during the contract's life. A contract attachment will state the beginning material defect rate; the commitment to quality improvement process during the contract period; the format of the quality evidence to be presented; and, the quality review schedule. It is intended that quality performance will become a negotiating element in future contractual agreements.

As you can see, quality evidence plays a large role in supplier development. It is similar to the situation in which we described data accuracy. You can't know which mountain you stand upon if you don't have the correct map. Quality evidence, such as charting, cause and effect diagrams, control charts, Pareto charts, histograms and data collection and correlation, are instrumental in the achievement of supplier certification. Later in this chapter, we will look more closely at Statistical Process Control (SPC) as a tool for suppliers enrolled in your certification program.

First, let's look at what levels of quality evidence you will find at a supplier's facility. The chart on page 54 begins with Level 3. A supplier at this level reflects little effort to change its level of quality. This company is still stuck within an inspection mentality as opposed to an understanding of its quality process. There is little use of statistics in such a company as a means for problem analysis and process control. Above all, a supplier at this level is unable to provide acceptable product quality evidence. He or she is not even literate in quality improvement and unaware of anything except traditional bromides handed down and accepted without question. Suppliers at this level often view supplier certification as an annoyance and not an opportunity.

At Level 2, the supplier has just entered school. Quality awareness and literacy is in its elementary stages. Quite simply, this level is comprised of learning stages and there can be much variation in the levels of quality comprehension suppliers exhibit. But, what distinguishes this level from Level 1 is that there is not, as of yet, mastery of the subject matter.

Level 2 suppliers have stated their commitment to quality and their effort to achieve TQC is obvious, if only in the growing stage. They have put personnel in place, generated plans, and have begun training their workers and management in the philosophy of TQC. This commitment must be exhibited, stated and believed fully by management in order for a supplier to reach this level. You will know it is true commitment if you see evidence of quality measurements being derived and used. Specifically, this means evidence of statistical training and applications used in process control and that the derived information is being used in a

SUPPLIER CHARACTERISTICS AND QUALITY AWARENESS

Level 3	Level 2	Level 1
Little effort to change quality levels	Quality awareness/literacy started	Management commitment to quality:
Inspection mentality	Management commitment stated	Published quality statement
Little use of statistics for problem analysis and process control	Quality effort obvious:	Training
Unable to provide acceptable evidence of product quality	Personnel in place	Quality councils
	Plan being generated	Process improvement plans
	Training being done	Established quality process in place
	Quality metrics being derived and used:	Quality metrics in use:
	Statistics training and applications used in process control	Cost of quality
	Quality evidence being gathered on process control	Control charts/statistics
	Prevention programs de fined and initiated	Measurement of defectives
		Improvement philosophy demonstrated
		Future quality goals in place
		Quality improvement process implemented
		Quality evidence available for product:
		Critical path process measuring
		Demonstrated performance
		Prevention-oriented quality process in use

feedback loop to improve process control. Such suppliers will also have defined and initiated prevention programs, thus showing they subscribe to a basic belief of JIT/TQC — *CURE THE DISEASE, DON'T JUST TREAT THE SYMPTOM.*

At the apex of our system is Level 1 in which the student has graduated and may indeed be able to teach you something about quality. Management commitment to quality is overt, manifesting itself as a published quality statement, extensive training programs, quality councils, and process improvement plans. In short, an established quality process is in place as are quality metrics like control charts and defect measurements. Furthermore, all quality evidence is available and structured in such a way that performance and product quality is immediately apparent to interested customers.

Perhaps most importantly, a Level 1 supplier demonstrates a commitment which stretches into the future. Quality goals and improvement processes are clearly stated as well. And even more strongly than Level 2, the orientation of quality processes is preventive. Quality is built into the product; it is not inspected for after the fact.

Supplier Certification

Quality at the source is what we are trying to achieve. But how do we get that quality? By entering into a partnership with a supplier which is based on trust and cooperation. The next question is: How do we get trust, cooperation, and quality from a supplier? The answer is Supplier Certification. We see this as a five-phase program in which you can think of yourself as a scientist. You gather facts, make a hypothesis, run your experiment, and use the results to reformulate your hypothesis. The phases in Supplier Certification are similar. Here, too, you gather facts about a supplier, you design quality improvement processes, you put them into practice, and then you audit and maintain the process based on the results which you are continuously gathering and interpreting.

In this program, then, you can think of yourself as a medical researcher who takes a patient and not only finds a cure, but finds means for the patient's continued well-being. You can think of this process as the compilation of a medical history, the implementation of a nourishing diet and a schedule of exercise, and the institution of regular check-ups. Your goal is to develop a partnership in which a healthy supplier will act according to the regimen of TQC and JIT.

PHASE ONE: History, Status, Documentation

The patient has entered your office. You wish to determine if this supplier is in good enough shape to work in a symbiotic relationship with your company. To determine if his or her company is "fit", you must assess the present health of quality processes and controls. There are a number of areas to probe:

First Article Inspection Status — Both you and the supplier conduct first article inspection of parts shipped to your company. You compare results in order to establish a common language.

Incoming Quality Control History — Now that you are both speaking about the same body, you can begin to identify types of rejects through a review of incoming history. This step works in conjunction with the next one.

Line Fallout — Quality problems will also help you identify errors on the production line as well. By reviewing the percentage of reject types, you can begin to isolate where the disease is located and what are some probable courses of action.

Part Documentation Review and Update — Since you are a researcher whose own health is important to the symbiotic relationship you hope to develop, you must make sure that the specs and drawings you send to the supplier are accurate. There are few things more annoying and eventually detrimental than writing out illegible "prescriptions" which the supplier must then fill or build.

Status Surveys — The remaining areas — Packaging Specifications/Method of Shipment, Production Tooling Status, Inspection Tooling Status, Delivery Performance — follow the same method of probing as the previous areas. You isolate the problem area, you identify the cause and you suggest "cures." But, you don't do this alone. Listen to your patient. Any good doctor does.

PHASE TWO: Supplier Program Review and Process Evaluation

You have started your research by talking with your supplier. To continue our analogy, it is as though you have communicated with the mind and sought out problems it perceived. The next step is to examine the body, that is, the supplier's plant and the systems which contribute to its quality health. Remember that you are not only a psychologist interested in the supplier's mind-set, but a physician interested in its biology, or the workings of its systems.

Obviously, this means a visit to the supplier's plant. That's right! You make house calls. While there, you make two principal examinations — one is a review of the supplier's manufacturing process and two is a survey of the supplier's quality process. Now, being a good doctor who wishes to make a correct diagnosis, you bring along colleagues. For example, buyer/planners, design engineers, production engineers, quality personnel. Evaluation by a multi-disciplined team means you will not overlook details and lose insight that only such an approach can bring. You can think of this approach as a built-in seeking of second and even third and fourth opinions.

Once these examinations are over, you will undoubtedly find some problems and weak areas which need strengthening. Your next step is to put all of your results in an Evaluation Memo which summarizes all corrective actions and constructs a time frame for their completion. At this point in your research, it is usually clear whether your supplier is willing to follow the course of quality health you are going to prescribe in conjunction with them. If the patient looks unwilling or incapable of helping themselves, end the certification process right here. You can't help those who won't help themselves.

PHASE THREE: Finalization

To this point, doctor and patient have worked closely. But, just as a psychologist makes ready the time for the eventual end of therapy, so too must suppliers be prepared to strike out on their own. This phase begins that process. First, you and the supplier must reach an agreement that all the courses of corrective action delineated in the Evaluation Memo have been followed. Second, you must agree on how to handle inspection of the supplier's product in the intermediate stage prior to full certification.

There are two ways to handle this time period:

1. Determine the required number of acceptable lots that must pass through your Incoming Inspection before the supplier is certified and has the quality and production processes in place to insure TQC and zero-defect products. The minimum of acceptability should be several consecutive lots.

2. Initiate source inspection if the past performance of the supplier seems to warrant it or if you lack sufficient inspection capability. Another alternative is to purchase source inspection from an outside service.

PHASE FOUR: Certification

This is what we have been working toward — a clean bill of health. The next step is to put into practice an inspection and monitoring program to maintain that health. You want to work toward a program which does not entail continuous attention, but uses statistical sampling. The result you seek with your suppliers is their conformance to TQC parameters.

Again, you pay attention to the areas of incoming inspection and process fall-out. Your task in conjunction with the supplier is to insure that the production line and incoming inspection (of course, there is no Receiving Inspection once the supplier is certified) have controls in place to properly identify rejects by part number and percentage. Then, you and the supplier can initiate corrective action once a problem is detected. Now we have achieved the most important part of Supplier Certification — the ability to cure the disease and not just treat the symptom. When a program is in place which subscribes to this maxim, then the supplier is qualified. Once qualified, acknowledge the achievement with a certificate or some type of ceremony. Continued good health is determined by high morale.

PHASE FIVE: On-going Audit and Maintenance

What is left for you now is a schedule of check-ups. If there are deviations from TQC, both you and the supplier need to be sure of how to detect them and how to get back on the path to health. You can accomplish this by doing random audits of incoming material and by keeping your documentation up-to-date.

A supplier can lose its qualified status as a result of lots being shipped having discrepancies with no immediate resolution. In this eventuality, you must alert the supplier with a Memo of Disqualification which outlines the problem and suggestions for how it can be solved. Requalification, for the most part, means repeating Phases Three and Four. Just remember that the path to quality health is gradual. That does not mean slow, but it does mean that you may experience setbacks. The difference is that you will know how to treat recurrences of quality disease.

Statistical Process Control

Statistical Process Control is part of the qualification process. SPC sets in place a monitoring system which insures that production processes at the supplier's plant will never deviate from making zero-defect parts. SPC, then, takes place in the supplier's environment, but teaching quality does not end there.

SPC is the brainchild of W. Edwards Deming who developed a 14-step approach for the achievement of Total Quality Control. We will first discuss these steps and our own **Essentials of Quality.** Then, we will discuss a five-point plan of implementation. Keep in mind, also, that Deming's approach provides a good outline for any problem-solving activity in your factory.

SPC is a powerful tool when used correctly. Too many customers are placing demands on suppliers to provide charts. Suppliers are charting all attributes and not just those which are critical. In developing a supplier, we should mutually review the critical characteristics and develop the criteria as to when the charts will be utilized in performing process capability at the supplier.

SPC is important to a supplier because it first forces them to determine if the process has the ability to produce the required quality. If so, then utilizing control charts keeps the process and quality in control. Our purpose in charting is to control the process and communicate the results. Simply providing control charts to the customer is not our objective.

THE DEMING APPROACH

1. INNOVATE — Allocate resources to fulfill the long-range needs of the company and the customer. The next quarterly dividend is not as important as the existence of your company five, ten or twenty years from now. One requirement of innovation is faith that there will be a future. Put resources into plans for product and service for the future, taking into account:

    • Possible materials, adaptability, probable cost
    • Method of production; possible changes in equipment
    • New skills required, and in what number?
    • Training and retraining of personnel
    • Training of supervisors
    • Cost of production
    • Performance in the hands of the user
    • Satisfaction of the user

2. LEARN THE NEW PHILOSOPHY — We will no longer accept defective material, material unsuited to the job, defective workmanship, and equipment out of order.

3. ELIMINATE DEPENDENCE ON MASS INSPECTION FOR QUALITY — Instead, depend on suppliers which use process control through statistical techniques. The purchaser is entitled to a supplier's control charts to assess critical characteristics of purchased material as evidence of quality, uniformity, and cost.

4. REDUCE THE NUMBER OF SUPPLIERS FOR THE SAME

ITEM— You will be lucky to find, for any item, one supplier who can furnish evidence of repeatable, dependable quality and who knows what his or her costs will be. Price has no meaning without evidence of quality. Demand and expect suppliers to use SPC and to furnish evidence that they do.

5. USE STATISTICAL TECHNIQUES TO IDENTIFY THE 2 SOURCES OF WASTE — Faults of the system, or common causes, account for 85%. Local faults account for 15%. Strive constantly to reduce this waste.

6. INSTITUTE BETTER TRAINING ON THE JOB — with the help of statistical methods.

7. PROVIDE SUPERVISION WITH USE OF STATISTICAL METHODS— Encourage use of these methods to identify which defects should be investigated for a solution. The aim of supervision is to help people do their job right.

8. DRIVE FEAR OUT OF THE ORGANIZATION — The economic loss resulting from fear to ask questions or report trouble is appalling.

9. REDUCE WASTE BY PUTTING TOGETHER A TEAM — Form a team from people who work on design, research, sales, and production.

10. ELIMINATE THE USE OF GOALS AND POSTED SLOGANS —They are an attempt to increase productivity. Such attempts, in the absence of quality control, will be interpreted by the work force as management's hope for a easy way out and as an indication that management has abandoned the job and have acknowledged their total inadequacy.

11. EXAMINE CLOSELY THE IMPACT OF WORK STANDARDS IN PRODUCTION — Work standards are exacting a heavy toll on the economy. There is a better way.

12. INSTITUTE ELEMENTARY STATISTICAL TRAINING — And do so on a broad scale. Thousands of people must learn simple, but powerful statistical methods.

13. INSTITUTE A VIGOROUS PROGRAM FOR RETRAINING PEOPLE— Teach them new skills, how to keep up with changes in materials, methods, design of product, and machinery.

14. MAKE MAXIMUM USE OF STATISTICAL KNOWLEDGE AND TALENT IN YOUR COMPANY — Statistical quality technology is a method which is transferable to different problems and circumstances. It does not consist of a set of procedures which are kept on file, ready for a specific application to this or that kind of product or process. **(1)**

The Deming approach makes a lot of sense. But what are these statistical techniques mentioned in the list and how do we show a supplier how to use them effectively?

The technique employed is a process control chart. It will chart a process in order to keep it under control. It's that easy to describe. But, if you went on to your shop floor and said, "We're going to use charts to monitor our process," you'll get a lot of blank stares. That's because you can't introduce SPC techniques without first doing some education and training. So, let's talk about this before we get into the actual charting.

We base education and training on what we call the **Essentials of Quality**. Without them, neither you or your supplier can successfully employ statistical techniques. They are an educational foundation upon which you and your supplier will build a training program for the application of SPC.

ESSENTIALS OF QUALITY

Management commitment and active participation
Total quality training for every employee
Design for reliability
Design for manufacturability
Conformance to specification
Develop processes and methods for error-free work
Use SPC
Implement a preventive maintenance program
Employee involvement in quality
Continuous reduction in part-to-part variation

The purpose of education is to make your company and the supplier's company aware of quality issues. The purpose of training is to teach ways to apply what you have learned. An effective training program in SPC has five training components:

Use verbal communication
Provide written instruction
Demonstrate with visual aids
Allow students to practice
Provide a memory key

These components are the framework in which you teach the specific rules for process control charting. In our example, the training components are the trusses and 2x4's on the concrete foundation of education. The specific rules can be likened to the sheetrock walls which finally define the shape of the house. The training components above reinforce quality issues through verbal discussion, written brochures and manuals, actual demonstrations and student practice. All these components are not merely taught, but are further reinforced with memory keys which can take the form of procedure sheets which are actually tacked on to walls or machines and which are clearly visible to workers as a jog for their memory.

As for specific rules relating to control charting, it is necessary to provide operators with four rules which will allow them to control quality. First, you let operators know what is a correct part and why. Second, you give them ways of determining if the part is right. Third, you give operators the means to determine a change over time in order to prevent defects. Fourth, you give instructions on how to adjust or change the process before defects occur.

Now you are ready to let operators benefit from the training by keeping statistical records of their machine's operation. These will take the form of a control chart. But, before operators at a supplier start using control charts, they must establish that the process is capable. We need to set some precontrol rules for a simple and effective method of allowing them to control the process. Given sample sizes of five parts for set-ups and two consecutive parts at regular intervals or continuous for run time, the precontrol rules say:

SET-UP: OK to run when all five results are inside the target area.

RUNNING: 1. If results are inside target area, continue to run.
2. As results tend toward control limits, operator may continue to run until more than one falls outside of control limits.
3. No parts are allowed to go beyond the limits and remain with good parts.

Results are tabulated on a control chart like the one depicted here for a machined steel rod whose limits are plus or minus .003 inches. Tests are conducted to determine where the upper and lower control limits are placed in order to insure with greater than 99% accuracy that only acceptable parts are produced.

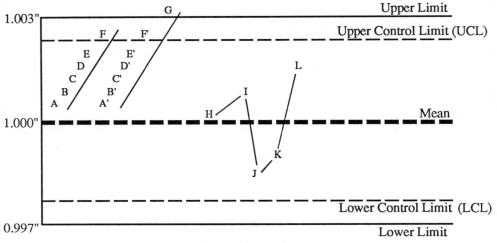

PROCESS CONTROL CHART

The operator of this particular machine which makes the rods would then begin to make parts as soon as five consecutive parts fall within the area between UCL and LCL. This would complete the set-up. Now the operator would begin the run. The first part (A) measures slightly more than 1 inch. B through E gradually deviate further from the mean, but in a predictable pattern. In this case, it would probably indicate that the cutting tool needed adjustment or that a whole new tool was needed. Repeated use throws original settings out of kilter as well as wearing down edges. Predictably, the sixth part (F) falls beyond the upper control limit. It is still, however, within acceptable tolerances. Therefore, the part is not rejected, but the process is calibrated to insure that the next part will follow the same pattern as depicted by A' through F'.

What happens when the operator measures a part that falls at G? The operator then physically separates the part from other produced pieces and STOPS the process. She calls over her supervisor or consults a troubleshooting guide to see why the process went wrong. She does not make another part until the disease is found and cured. She does not treat the symptom and hope for the best.

Finally, what does it mean when an operator charts measurements which appear like H through L? They are all in the control limits, all perfectly acceptable. But, they do not depict a predictable pattern. Such a chart indicates that the process is out of control. Here, too, the operator stops her run and finds out why the machine is performing erratically.

As we have said before, JIT and TQC give the operator responsibility and authority. These charts clearly show how this works in the real world. Each operator is responsible for charting the machine's process and has the authority to stop the machine when parts fall out of predictable patterns or beyond acceptable limits.

If your supplier has SPC in place, you can be assured of two things — zero-defect parts and, most importantly, a process which will continue to produce zero-defect parts. That is why SPC is such an important part of Purchasing's role in procuring quality products.

However, it doesn't stop here. There must be on-going education and a program to promote quality. Quality must be a way of life or, as Ford says, "Quality is Job 1." A poorly designed product fights an uphill battle, maybe even a losing battle, against quality. If you are going to make it right the first time, you must design it right the first time.

CHAPTER FIVE: The Engineering Interface

The Purchasing employee who has a total business concept not only looks outside the company at suppliers for improvement, but also keenly regards the inside of the company for ways to reduce costs and eliminate wastes. In short, this employee should consider the entire company as the domain in which he or she seeks to improve performance. A baseball team, for example, has a general manager who is responsible for the team's performance on the field. He employs scouts to evaluate players on other teams or in the farm leagues. In a certain sense, Purchasing Departments are like these scouts. They go out and evaluate players for which the team may want to trade. To carry our analogy one step further, however, we must add that Purchasing Departments are also part batting coach or pitching instructor. They take the resources on hand and shape them into competitive players.

Now that you have acted like the scout and established a Supplier Certification Program, it is time to look inward and take the role of coach. Just as you have built good relationships with suppliers, so should you build bridges between Purchasing and the disciplines of engineering. As you will see, the work done with suppliers will pay off here in many ways. And, like any good manager of a team, you will be a coach and a scout at the same time. Interfacing with your suppliers and with your Engineering department are done simultaneously, not sequentially.

We have noticed, in seminars presented around the country, the presence of distrust between Engineering and Purchasing departments. Often it hides behind a friendly antagonism as if the two were rivals in some local softball league. Pride in one's area of work is not to be diminished, but at the same time it should not dictate actions, or lack of action. Engineering and Purchasing are not rivals. Both departments work for the same company, not against each other. Basically, the antagonism rises between two work environments. Engineering necessarily designs in an ideal environment; Purchasing buys from a world littered with problems.

But, this does not mean the two can't come together. Since we are talking about Purchasing in this book, we will place the burden of bridge-building on that department. It can start very easily, with a simple explanation of the benefits to be derived from a symbiotic relationship. This symbiosis can be aptly described a follows:

> "The prices paid for production materials and the costs
> to fabricate them are inextricably related to their
> specifications ... materials must be both economical to
> procure and economical to fabricate." **(1)**

We know these areas are important because of the comments we hear all over the country in all types of businesses. We hear Engineering asking for input from Purchasing in selecting economic alternatives, in evaluating supplier strengths and weaknesses and in identifying source problems. Others note how suppliers can help Engineering standardize parts and how Purchasing can track down sources, get samples and prices, and reduce lead times.

All this activity centers around a core in which Purchasing, Engineering and suppliers seek "real-world" ways to solve problems. This is not an easy task, but it is an absolutely essential one. Quite simply, it requires that Purchasing build bridges between the participants. Certainly the vitality, and perhaps even the survival, of your business depends on open avenues.

Design and Engineering Teams

It's apparent, then, that one tackles this problem with a team approach in which Engineering, Marketing, Purchasing and Suppliers sit down with each other. Early involvement of all the participants is the key and, as a survey points out, this is happily becoming more true. In this survey, conducted in the mid 1980s, *Purchasing Magazine* asked Purchasing Managers how often their departments received advance notice of design plans. Those responding "very often" and "fairly often" improved from 60% to 70% in the four years between surveys; a definite improvement, but still short of what is needed to stay competitive.

A team approach to design would of course eliminate the question of when Purchasing becomes involved, because they are always involved. Here, we want to stress the importance of involving Marketing right up front as well. All too often, we encounter the following scenario at seminars and with clients:

> The company is ready to design a new product. Some preliminary work has been done between Engineering and Production. Perhaps Marketing has even begun to sell the new product. The problem arises when com- panies introduce the product into the marketplace and begin promoting it before anyone has seriously considered its design. The reasoning goes like this: "We have to hurry up and release this product into the marketplace or else our competition will gain a significant foothold on market share." Coleco's home computer, Adam, is an excellent example.

We aren't singling out Marketing or Sales as the villain. The fact is that mid-stream changes and hasty decision-making can come from anywhere. Indeed, it may ultimately be top management's fault for not implementing good design management practices. Below are the common reasons for failure which we have derived from our experience:

COMMON REASONS FOR DESIGN FAILURE

1. Excessive Changes
2. Poor Design System
3. Producibility Not Considered
4. No Design Development Integration
5. We Lack:
   Manufacturing Interface
   Quality Assurance Interface
   Marketing Interface
   Supplier Interface
   Purchasing Interface
   Adequate Testing

If any one quality characterizes this list, it is the absence of clearly identified routes with destinations marked along the way. Instead, we have a departure point and an arrival point with a vast, amorphous area in between as the maps of Africa used to show. These areas were called "Uncharted Territories," but uncharted to whom? Certainly not to the people who lived there. The point is that you have to explore these areas, talk to the natives, open up the territory. Ask yourself if you would build a railroad across land that had not been carefully surveyed. Of course not, and so, above all else, good design management requires clear goals, or charted territory.

Other design management requirements are:

   • **Keep the design as simple as possible.**

   • **Complete the design on time.**

With a Design team in place, these requirements are not

impossible, because with the team comes design integration. No one person can have their finger on all the pulses (Purchasing, Quality, Marketing, Production, Suppliers, etc.) which make up the living body of design just as one doctor can not perform a major operation without the input of colleagues or the assistance of a staff. The rule for a Design team is very simple — sit down and talk with each other. You will certainly learn of each other's requirements.

When we use the term Design Team, we have in mind a broad-based group which not only includes Design Engineering, but Industrial Engineering, Manufacturing Engineering, Facilities Engineering as well as Purchasing. Such a group will go beyond design considerations, however, and involve itself with tooling, quality, supplier selection and certification, learning curves, reduction of set-up times, work simplification, and value analysis. It is the last item, value analysis, which forms something like a philosophy, an overall set of rules for lowering costs and reducing waste.

Value Analysis

Simply put, Value Analysis says that if costs can be reduced without reducing the quality of the product, then we can be more productive. It also states that the whole workforce should be involved in this process. Value Analysis can be thought of as a tool to reach management goals.

Value Analysis has two stages. The first stage looks at the design and the second looks at individual parts applications. Each stage has a set of questions which act as guidelines to open discussion. The first set of questions is as follows:

VALUE ANALYSIS — STAGE ONE
Design Analysis

1. Can any part be eliminated without impairing the operation of the complete unit?
2. Can the design of the part be simplified to reduce its basic cost?

3. Can the design of the part be changed to permit the use of simplified and less costly production methods?
4. Can less expensive but equally satisfactory materials be used in the part? **(2)**

This list is not intended to be exhaustive. It is a start, hopefully, to brainstorming sessions in which all participants will air their views. Open and honest discussion is essential to this type of analysis. It helps you avoid a highly detrimental practice we call "lobbing grenades." It works like this: You design something, initiate a procedure, or implement a system and then toss your idea or plan over the wall of your cubicle to the next department. Most of the time it explodes in that person's face. Why? Simply because we never expected it and because it is completely at odds with the way we run our departments.

Take the time to engineer it right the first time. Use these questions to defuse the grenades.

VALUE ANALYSIS — STAGE TWO
Item Checklist

First, determine the function of the item, then determine:

1. Can the item be eliminated?
2. If the item is not standard, can a standard item be used?
3. If it is a standard item, does it completely fit the application or is it a misfit?
4. Does the item have greater capacity than required?
5. Can the weight be reduced?
6. Is there a similar item in inventory that could be substituted?
7. Are closer tolerances specified than are necessary?
8. Is unnecessary machining performed on the item?
9. Are unnecessarily fine finishes specified?
10. Is "commercial quality" specified? (Commercial quality is usually most economical.)

11. Can you make the item more cheaply in your plant? if you are making it now, can you buy it for less?
12. Is the item properly classified for shipping purposes to obtain lowest transportation rates?
13. Can cost of packaging be reduced?
14. Are suppliers being asked for suggestions to reduce cost? **(3)**

We think a fifteenth step should be added: Are there any other ways to reduce costs?

This second list originally appeared in a pamphlet prepared by the Value Analysis Standardization Committee, chaired by Martin S. Erb, of the National Association of Purchasing Management (NAPM). It quite clearly shows the importance of Purchasing's impact on engineering questions.

Engineering and Suppliers

Purchasing has another role to play as a switchboard between suppliers and engineering. Valuable information which can help the design process forms a two-way conversation between the two areas. Purchasing's job is to link up the two lines.

In the communication from engineering to suppliers, we advocate that anything Engineering departments do in-house, can and should be done in the supplier's house. Just as we recommend involving other functional areas in the design process, so we recommend involving Industrial Engineering, Manufacturing Engineering, Quality Engineering and Design Engineering in supplier selection. First of all, Engineering can assist in the evaluation of Value Analysis ideas from suppliers. Second, it can aid Purchasing in the evaluation of suppliers' plant layouts. Third, it can assess process, or the flow of material; inspection, both tooling and process; and the control of quality, material and lead time in the supplier's plant.

This should not be an overly difficult task for the various engineering departments. As we have said, these are evaluations which they are called upon to do everyday in their own company.

Obviously, this is their area of expertise and to ignore this capacity is foolhardy at best. They are very likely to locate problems that were overlooked by people without well-developed engineering skills.

On the other side of the two-way street between engineering and suppliers, that is, the path of communication from the suppliers to engineering, it would be equally foolhardy to ignore suggestions from suppliers. Suppliers are also experts in their field.

Purchasing Magazine ran an article with a title which neatly sums up our emphasis on suppliers and the flow of information — "Better-forged links bring in better designs: purchasing's enhanced position in the information loop maximizes suppliers' engineering assistance." **(4)**

Unfortunately, it is not the norm in U.S. manufacturing to encourage this information loop. The *Purchasing Magazine* survey we referred to earlier in this chapter cites another result which is either discouraging or heartening, depending on your view. The question which the magazine asked was: How often does Purchasing call on suppliers for design aid? Those who answered "always" rose from 8% to 10%. "Very often" and "fairly often" went from 67% to 76%. **(5)**

The good news is that we are moving in the right direction; the bad news is that we have a long way to go. Perhaps the best way to proceed along this path to full and open cooperation between departments and suppliers is to form a permanent link between Engineering and Purchasing. We are advocating that Purchasing assign buyers to Engineering to act not only as liaisons, but as resident experts. A buyer can educate Engineering about the role of Purchasing. Both Engineering and Purchasing seek to find the best "design." Such a buyer can also help Engineering evaluate suppliers and their products.

Think how valuable the latter can be to Engineering. No longer will an engineer requisition a part that has an impossible lead time or exorbitant costs or ask for a part from a supplier you know to make only 75 to 80 good parts out of every 100. Nobody should expect an engineer to be as proficient in these areas. But, what you should expect is an engineer and a buyer who are both smart enough to listen to each other and to benefit from each other's area of expertise.

Here is a list of the ways in which a buyer can assist Engineering:

1. Bring players together.
2. Negotiate price, delivery, quality and quantity.
3. Act as the team catalyst.
4. Provide alternatives.

Engineering Interfaces

Now that we have been introduced to the Purchasing/Engineering team, let's look at the players — Design Engineering, Industrial Engineering, Manufacturing Engineering, Quality Engineering and Facilities Engineering.

Basically, Design Engineering is responsible for product development and improvement. Design works closely with Marketing which gauges the buying trends of the market place. The objective is to maintain a competitive edge. A key player in this process is Purchasing. As a member of the Purchasing department, you should be asking yourself how to procure quality parts within cost considerations every time a product changes or is introduced.

Sometimes, it is even necessary to determine whether the parts are available from any source. Producibility is directly related to design. If the new design is overly complicated or contains impossible specifications, then suppliers will not be able to produce the part. This is where it is necessary to get Design and the supplier together, so that they can work out the problems. In this way, they can learn from each other.

Starting and supporting this interaction is Purchasing's forte, especially with a Supplier Certification Program in place. It is obvious that Purchasing can provide Design Engineering with a great deal of information about which suppliers are reliable and which ones are state-of-the-art. All because Purchasing has built a solid foundation of credibility with suppliers.

Industrial Engineering is principally concerned with flow in the JIT environment. Whether a manufacturer should use an S-shaped or U-shaped production line is really not as important as using a line which works best in a particular facility. How do you know if it is the best method? There are two very simple rules:

1. Material never travels backwards.
2. There will be enough time in production for the operator to complete a task with 100% acceptable quality.

Obviously, from these two basic rules, there will grow a whole set of work standards. Traditionally, Industrial Engineering set these standards. In a JIT factory, first line supervisors should set them because they are far more familiar with what works and what doesn't. It's just the old team concept again: Involve people in decisions and they can work miracles.

One of Manufacturing Engineering's primary roles is to consider the producibility of new products or changes, as we have mentioned. In that role, they must be involved with Design right from the very beginning of the design process.

Another role for Manufacturing centers around tooling which should not be overlooked as an opportunity to improve. Here, too, what can be done in-house, can also be done in the suppliers' factory. Manufacturing should look at the tooling and set-up efficiency of suppliers. We will discuss this area in more detail later when we look at reducing set-up times.

Facilities Engineering manages the areas of building size, air conditioning/heating, lighting and music. These environmental considerations have a demonstrable effect on workers and the quality of products they produce. For example, in the Kawasaki plant in Nebraska, we improved working conditions by piping in rock music. This was appropriate since the average age of a line worker was 22 years old. It would have been counterproductive in that environment to play Classical music.

Learning Curves

The learning curve is not a new concept, but it is of particular importance to JIT where improvement is an on-going commitment. It has been referred to as a "commonsense observation that the unit cost of a new product decreases as more units of the product are made." (6)

As workers repeat a task, they obviously become more adept and faster. This means more units can be produced in a given time period. At the same time, they do their work more accurately which reduces the number of mistakes. This, too, increases the number of units produced in a time period.

The beauty of learning curves is that with the on-going commitment, training and education of JIT, you can always expect to see improvement. This commitment grows as the various teams work on problems.

One small warning about learning curves: When changes are first introduced, you may see a rise in costs as workers "unlearn" old methods. Once the new replaces the old, however, in the minds of workers, there will be a sharp and accelerating reduction in costs which will surpass previous standards. JIT looks for this long-range benefit and does not become frustrated with any short-term fluctuations as long as they are within expected ranges.

Of course, the learning curve shows the best results when you simplify the work at hand. In a way, a factory is like a well-constructed short story. A short story should focus on one character or one event. There should be no elements in the story that do not advance the themes, plot, or character. A writer accomplishes this task by organizing along the guidelines of simplicity and elegance. So, too, with a factory. Your plant should focus on the production of those products for which you have the expertise, material, and equipment. Particular attention should be paid to material flow, operation processes, people and machines, and employee activity. Your guiding principle in controlling this process flow goes by the name of work simplification.

Work Simplification

There are five steps in work simplification. First, you select an area to improve. Selection is based on visibility, payback, and impact which can be determined with Pareto charts. In other words, look for the 20% which affects 80% of your costs of inventory or which accounts for 80% of your problems. These areas are candidates for improvement. Next, you want to narrow down this list to that area which will demonstrate clear results so that other departments in your company will readily see the benefits of change.

Second, get all the facts; make a process flow chart which forces you to break a task down into its components. Then, you can examine each activity and begin to evaluate it in terms of eliminating, changing or combining sequences, places or people. This chart is at the core of work simplification since it allows you to list possibilities.

Details of Present or Proposed Method	Operation	Transport	Inspection	Delay	Storage	Distance	Quantity	Time	Eliminate	Combine	Sequence	Place	Person	Improve	Notes

We have found that the use of video cameras is invaluable in gathering information about the different areas of process flow. As you view your "home movies," you are looking for ways to economize motion and to arrange the workplace and tooling.

We have all seen the seven-year-old judo student who can flip his 200-pound teacher. The child can do this because he uses only those motions which contribute to the laying out of his instructor. Also, the child uses the larger man's weight against himself.

These two principles of physics are similar to what we want to achieve in motion economy. The idea is to have no wasted motions, to use gravity and momentum to our advantage, to keep a smooth and constant rhythm, and to use the least amount of effort. These same attributes dictate workplace arrangement and tool use. Anything which eliminates strain, positioning, and movement to obtain tools or material is what we should look for.

To give you a more precise idea of what to look for and what to improve, we have included the following suggestions for motion economy:

- Begin each element simultaneously with both hands.
- Use simultaneous arm motions in opposite symmetrical directions.
- End each element simultaneously.
- Use hand motions of lowest classification.
- Keep motion paths within normal range.
- Avoid sharp changes in direction with smooth, curved motions.
- Slide or roll; don't lift or carry.
- Locate tools and materials in proper sequence.
- Use method with fewest work elements, shortest time, least fatigue.
- Relieve hands with foot pedals whenever practical.
- Use rhythm to increase output and reduce fatigue.
- Use vice instead of hand holding; frees hand to move pieces.
- Provide foot operated ejectors; remove pieces completed.
- Use gravity drop delivery to dispose of finished piece.
- Shorten all transports and provide gravity feed hoppers.
- Pre-position tools for quick grasp.
- Pre-position product for next operation.
- Locate machine controls for convenience, ease and safety.
- Design workplace for height, posture, back-rest, foot-rest.
- Provide pleasant working conditions: light, temperature, noise, color, etc.

In Step Three, we interpret the process flow chart by challenging every fact you have gathered. We all have heard the story about the cub reporter on a newspaper who must answer, in the first paragraph of his story, the following questions: who, what, where, when and how. Your job in this step is not that easy. Not only do you have to ask each of these questions about every detail, but you have to ask "why?" after each question. For example: "When does this activity occur?" "Why does it occur then?" "Who does this activity?" "Why does he or she do it and not somebody else?"

Nothing, not one procedure, in the plant is sacred. Growth, improvement, cost reduction, call it what you will, only comes when you begin challenging accepted practices. Now, we are not suggesting that you become a radical and burn the factory to the ground, so you can start all over. We are suggesting that you take your questions and answers and find what you can eliminate, combine or change.

Once a process flow chart has been developed, you also can do a process design such as the one below. Here you can see the design before and after design changes were made. Notice the reduction in complexity.

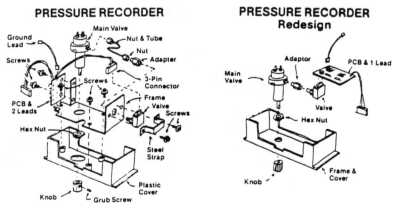

PRESSURE RECORDER

PRESSURE RECORDER Redesign

Courtesy Boothroyd Dewhurst, Inc.
Wakefield, RI

In step four of the five steps of work simplification, we use our matrix and our challenges to develop a preferred method. The last step is to install this method and monitor it which, like all good JIT activities brings us full circle and places us in the position to start another round of improvement.

Work simplification is not only applied to the reduction of parts and machine operations, but to people as well. When human beings are involved, there are several important things to remember:

Employees are not machines.

Employees are a resource.

Tasks which are too simple can be just as counterproductive as difficult tasks.

When changes are proposed, the question most asked by workers is "What's in it for me?" This is why we stress involving them in team reviews of any work simplification projects. We suggest that there should be about five people on such a team: an industrial engineer, the person(s) doing the work, the person(s) affected by the work and someone who isn't involved at all. Often, it is this last person, with his or her "dumb" questions, who can best cut through patterns which have been ingrained. Such a person should always ask "why?". "Why do you do this? Why do you need that?"

Reducing Set-up Times

You can think of set-up reduction as a subset of work simplification. The steps for both are similar. The intent of set-up reduction is to reduce production set-up times in order to support a movement toward small lot sizes and an overall improvement in productivity. We must also remember that set-up time is defined as the time between the last good part of the previous set-up and the first good part of the subsequent set-up.

There are two related processes in set-up reduction:

1. Setting and tooling of equipment, and
2. Determination of lot sizes.

The two are interrelated in the following ways:

1. Smaller lot sizes make it necessary for faster change-overs of equipment.
2. Smaller lot sizes require more set-ups which places an emphasis on zero lot excess. Zero lot excess means JIT delivery to the line and better procurement decisions based on need and quality rather than price alone.
3. Long set-ups mean long runs which translates into more WIP inventory as stock builds up before being worked on by the next operation.
4. Reduced set-ups mean shorter runs which translates into less WIP inventory as stock is worked on more quickly by the next operation.

In the ideal JIT/TQC shop floor, set-ups are so fast that lot sizes of one can be run. In other words, a machine makes one part based on demand and sends it on to the next machine. The first machine then sets up for the next part to be worked on. To obtain levels approaching that ideal requires a persistent effort on one machine at a time. Improvements should be simple and adhere to the rule of common sense. No $50,000 *whatchamacallits* to be bolted onto a drill press. We have heard of one set-up that was reduced by using a yardstick marked with nail polish to designate standard lengths. Lastly, set-up reduction can initiate design changes — a new size screw perhaps that is the same size as other screws used elsewhere. The job of Purchasing is to get suppliers involved in set-up reduction. And that brings us to the beginning of how to reduce set-ups.

The first step is to *use the users*. These are the people most familiar with machines on the shop floor, not necessarily engineers.

The second step is to *create a team*, consisting of a group leader and technical support that will back up workers and tell them if the proposed changes are sound. Of course, ideas can and should flow the other way as well. Shop floor people should have the authority and responsibility to assist the technical group. The team as a whole should have the authority and responsibility to go to the roots of problems and eliminate those causes. In other words, to use a popular phrase, they should have ownership in what they do.

The third step is to *analyze the set-up*. This step breaks down into four sub-steps:

1. Allocate the proper amount of set-up time so as to avoid producing inferior parts. Identify individual steps in the process in order to determine the most appropriate amount of set-up time to be eliminated.

2. Ask yourself what set-up steps are external (can be done while machine is running) and internal (cannot be done while machine is running). Can you begin setting up for the next operation while the prior one is still running? Can the set-up step be done as preparation before the machine is running or as clean-up after the machine is running? If it can be done externally, do so. Next, ask yourself if there is anything that is done with the machine stopped that can be done while the machine is running. If so, then change the set-up so that the formerly internal operation is now external. The point of this sub-step is to reduce the amount of down-time in a set-up.

3. Some of the time spent getting the new set-up to run is adjustment. This is the next area in which to look for reductions. Find ways to position tools or dies in one motion. Getting the equipment for a new job in the right position should not take inordinate amounts of time. Design set-ups so that equipment is self-position-ing. One method is to convert from infinitely adjust-able measurements to some kind of mechanical stop since most machines and equipment only use a very few of the infinite number of positions available. Finally, once a position is set, standardize it for as many set-up operations as possible.

   Also, and this bears repeating, don't consider a set-up reduced until you make the product right the first

time. Running parts through until you get a good one
is not reducing adjustment time.
4. Lastly, observe your clamping and unclamping operations. If you lose time in this area, find methods that
require less time. Instead of threaded bolts, consider
using levers, cam-action clamps, pins or wedges.
   Again, your effort should be concentrated on
finding methods that require only one or two motions
and that eliminate the need for tools. (7)

There is a "cost" side to engineering and JIT purchasing. Since
we emphasize total cost, it will require a new orientation between
Purchasing and Finance. This new emphasis appeared in the
Value Analysis list above — Is it better to make or to buy? Your
team will need more input than can be gathered from specifications or bills of material to answer this question. Where this input
comes from and how it is obtained and used is the subject of the
next chapter.

CHAPTER SIX: Financial Implications of JIT Purchasing

So far, we have emphasized the establishment of a foundation of good relations with various departments within the company and with suppliers. Upon these foundations, you will build bridges for the free and easy exchange of ideas which will improve quality, reduce costs and eliminate wastes. Although this bridge-building will not be without its difficulties, turf wars and other ego battles, it will link people and departments who have the same goal — the production of goods for sale to customers.

But, all too often, when it comes to building a bridge toward the domain of the Finance department, people forget about common goals. Suddenly, it is not the team, but "us" against "them." After all, the reasoning goes, these are the people who use methods developed in the early twentieth century and who never get out to the factory floor. Their shoulders are hunched from adding columns of numbers, and so on and so on. In other words, they aren't one of us. We may get angry at an engineer, but at least that person does what we perceive as "real work." All Finance seems to do is tell us what we can't do and build fences of financial restraints to make us feel penned in.

"If only they understood!" is the constant lament.

It may be trite to say, but bridge-building starts on both sides when there is distrust. Unless you like constant battling, you had better include Finance very early in your movement toward JIT Purchasing. Forming this link with Finance is as much everybody's responsibility as it is theirs. It is even more important in JIT Purchasing where, as we shall see, some of the old methods of financial accounting must be replaced.

This is because JIT Purchasing is no longer simply concerned with buying goods at the lowest price. Its new role is concerned with quality, delivery and total cost. Indeed, it may mean buying a more expensive item (that is, a higher-priced item) since the total cost may actually be less than the lower-priced item.

There is nothing surprising in the above example, but for companies who measure themselves with traditional yardsticks, a

Purchasing Manager who pays the highest price has been put behind the eight ball. How can he or she justify this action to the Finance Department when performance is measured by standards developed in the early part of this century? According to the authors of *Relevance Lost*,**(1)** accounting practices have not been changed since 1905. With this in mind, it is no wonder we are besieged by traditional constraints which affect performance measurement and correct decision-making.

In this chapter, we will look at how bridge-building can bring you not only into the present, but into the future.

Financial Analysis

When Peter L. Grieco, Jr. worked at Digital Equipment Corporation, he wrote a memorandum stating the following need for the Materials department at DEC:

"I have spent some time analyzing the needs of the Plant Materials function as it relates to financial assistance. I am requesting one (1) full-time Financial Analyst to be included in the Plant Material Staff to assist and recommend financial advice to the Material group."

This financial analyst is the bridge between Purchasing and Finance, just as the buyer/planner and the purchasing person in Engineering were bridges. The job description which he wrote for this position was lengthy. Most importantly, it explicitly stated that the job should include what was listed, but not be limited to that list. Again, this reflects our current belief that work should be defined by function and not by department or any other artificial structure. Consequently, we have changed the job title and description to fit more closely this person's functions. As you can see, we are asking that the person who builds the bridge between Finance and Purchasing to wear three hats.

BUYER/PLANNER/FINANCIAL ANALYST
Job Description

BUDGETS

Coordinate budget process with acquisition cost centers and interface with accounting (plant, corporate and supplier) regarding acquisition allocations and charges to materials. Reconcile value of shipments with customers and reconcile transfers of materials within plant. Establish a policy of reduced paperwork for Purchasing.

STANDARDS

Act as coordinator between businesses and purchasing and between purchasing and accounting. Analyze make/buy decisions and establish reviews prior to the process of establishing total cost objectives.

PHYSICAL INVENTORY

Determine all variances and spending related to material acquisition and be responsible for cost center charges and journal voucher entries. Determine costs of acquiring certain classes of materials and establish overhead rates for cost centers. Monitor inventory levels and shipments on a daily/weekly basis. Resolve accounts payable and receivable problems. Coordinate and forecast quarterly spending with acquisition cost center managers and control inventory reporting by product (weekly) to insure meeting plant goals for inventory turns.

PURCHASING

Audit the procurement system to insure contract awards meet company standards. Evaluate contract proposals and negotiation strategies. Serve as the financial adviser in all areas affecting Purchasing.

GENERAL

Review all material-related financial data and assist plant purchasing personnel with financial planning. Review long-range inventory strategy. Recommend financial advise as requested.

As you can see, this is no simple job. Notice, however, that the position emphasizes those very qualities which we have associated with JIT Purchasing — total cost, inventory control, and financial planning based on actual demand. In other words, the person you hire to be your financial analyst will be working within a system which supports his or her functions. There will be no more of the "us" against "them" attitude we mentioned at the beginning of this chapter.

Total Cost

One of the most important responsibilities of the financial analyst is to move away from a dependence on price analysis as the major criterion for determining product costs. Cost analysis will augment, and even replace, price analysis in JIT Purchasing. This is because cost analysis examines all costs involved in the process of manufacturing products, where as price analysis uses the seller's price without examining or evaluating the separate elements of cost and profit which make up the price. JIT Purchasing relies on a total cost approach based on this formula:

**TOTAL COST =
VARIABLE COSTS + FIXED COSTS + SEMIVARIABLE COSTS**

It should be noted that cost analysis has advantages over Purchase Price Variance (PPV). This method, in which Purchasing is measured against a standard cost set once a year, does not look at total cost, just price. It forces the buyer to purchase based on price rather than cost.

As you can see, we are returning to the formulas discussed in Chapter 1. There, we said that under traditional practices, we raise selling prices as costs increase in order to maintain the profit margin. Thus, we get this equation:

PROFIT = SELLING PRICE - COST

But in JIT Purchasing, we do a little algebra on the equation and come up with this:

SELLING PRICE = PROFIT + COST

Now, the price is set. In order to maintain or increase the profit margin, we must cut costs. In JIT Purchasing, cost reduction is everybody's job. Since the function of Finance is to be concerned with all costs, it's rather obvious that they will have an instrumental role in cost reductions.

Why is this true? Why is a system based on total cost much

more realistic and accountable? Why are companies reluctant to discontinue PPV as a total cost formula? There are two interrelated reasons. One is the fact that production is based on the Theory of One. An operator on a production line or a work station only uses as much material as is needed to build to the demand set by the operator or station in front of them. This, too, is built into the system. Consequently, there won't be any material floating around in the plant simply because there is no demand for it. Secondly, what material is in the plant contributes directly to the production of an end product, not to inventory carrying costs, not to time lost in receiving areas, not to expediting, not to late deliveries, and so on. Thus, financial control becomes a much simpler task as we focus on cost improvement.

Two more areas in which Purchasing can aid in reducing costs are elimination of set-up and acquisition costs. As previously outlined, this will entail implementing a set-up time reduction program (detailed in a forthcoming book from PT Publications), the use of systems contracts, and partnerships with suppliers.

Whatever the area, the following steps will be used by Purchasing:

9-STEP COST IMPROVEMENT METHOD

1. Identify Targets and Opportunities
2. Describe Them in Detail
3. Identify and Define Possible Problems
4. Set Objectives and Goals
5. Gather Facts and other Related Information and Analyze the Data
6. Determine Solutions
7. Evaluate Solutions and Alternatives
8. Implement Techniques to Solve Problems
9. Evaluate and Measure Results

The team, working with the financial analyst, will go through a familiar JIT cycle. The cycle begins by identifying cost targets. We will cover some of these targets in the section that follows. For now, just remember that you will begin in areas where there are demonstrable and visible results.

Second, you will describe the targets. The aim here is to note all costs, apparent and hidden, which are associated with the target.

Third, define the problems you are experiencing within these areas so that, fourth, you can set objectives. As with other areas of JIT, the rule of halves applies here as well. That is, you should seek to reach your goal by reaching a point half way between where you start and where you want to be. Once achieved, the new point becomes half the remaining distance to the goal.

Fifth, gather facts which will enable you to suggest possible solutions and analyze the data. Coming up with these hypotheses is the sixth step.

Seventh, evaluate your solutions. This is where the team becomes vitally important. Any solution you choose will have effects throughout the company. Have people on hand who can tell you how it will affect the operations and procedures in their individual departments. Of course, some areas are more greatly affected than others. Therefore, it is not necessary to have the whole company sit down and debate the merits and demerits of a proposed solution. Each company will find an optimum size for the team and a most effective make-up.

Eighth, implement the solution which the team has determined to be the most effective at cutting costs. Needless to say, the implementation, itself, must be cost-effective as well.

Ninth and last, evaluate the results of your implementation and either try another solution if results aren't as planned or move on to the next target point, if you have been successful.

Cost improvements can be either short-term or long-term. The following would be typical of a short-term cost improvement program:

Layoffs
Dead wood removal
Reduced overtime
No salary increases

Salary decreases
Reduced preventive maintenance
Reduced R&D
Scrapping of non-essential programs
Raised production standards
More frequent ordering
Lower quality standards

Some of the above are quite obviously detrimental to the continued vitality of a company. Shrinking R&D budgets or lowering quality standards, for example, may save money in the short run, but robs the future to pay for the present. Shortsighted actions of this sort are synonymous with "crisis management." And because crisis management usually shows a lack of a commitment toward excellence, long-term cost improvements, which are far-sighted, are inherently superior.

We often explain this as the difference between being a fire fighter and a fire chief. Fire fighters react by running around the company putting out brush fires. Fire chiefs seek out ways to prevent fires, just like Smokey the Bear. So, if you want to save the environment you work in, then think ahead and follow the 9-step cost improvement method at the beginning of this section.

In order to achieve success with this method, it will be necessary for you to set up a cost accounting system which incorporates the measurement of variances against standard costs, not prices. The key element in long-term cost improvement is the analysis of past performance and the directing of future actions. Albert Einstein once said that the division of time into past, present and future is an illusion. We would agree, that is, in the sense that each division is affected by the other two. What you plan to do in the present depends upon what you have done in the past and what you plan to do in the future.

Identify Cost Targets

The cost improvement framework will help you identify a number of targets requiring your attention. We will briefly describe some of these below. In no way is this list meant to be inclusive, but as an aid which will help you to identify your own. Although we find that many companies (whether large or small, whether food processors or manufacturers of office furniture) have similar problems, we also realize that the dynamics of your particular situation will have a great impact on your solutions. That is why it so important to use a team to understand the dynamics of cost improvement.

TYPICAL COST TARGETS

1. Labor
2. Inventory
3. Safety and Preventive Maintenance
4. Scrap, Rework and Quality
5. Energy, Equipment and Facilities
6. Time Management and Paperwork

The list begins with labor. Typical cost issues under this heading are salaries, fringes, absenteeism, and turnover after training. Next comes inventory. Issues here are carrying costs, distribution, warehousing, and cost of purchased materials.

You should also not overlook the costs of accidents. Proper safety procedures and preventive maintenance are essential to the reduction of lost time resulting from workers injuring themselves. Although there is no quantifiable measure for morale, except perhaps in productivity, it is clear that a safe workplace not only helps to create an atmosphere of teamwork, but also reduces scrap and improves quality.

Scrap, rework, and quality each deserve to be designated as cost targets in their own right as well. We mention the relationship between quality and safety in order to demonstrate the web which connects one cost issue to another. As in other areas of JIT, touching the web in one spot has repercussions in other spots. The team is there to search out all possible effects.

While we are still on the factory floor, don't neglect the areas of energy, equipment, and facilities as targets. The Far East, which is not blessed as we are with abundant resources, has been pressured to make dramatic improvements here. Part of the team's job will be to forecast where future constraints will occur that may have deleterious effects on your company.

The last few areas are more people-related, that is, those items which people use to help them do their job. In this list, we have telephone service, office supplies, time management, meetings, and paperwork. Although you may say that each of these areas has a small effect, their sum can be considerable. It would be like telling a race car driver to ignore a few protruding screws or door handles on his automobile. One screw may not cause much drag, but a lot of them combined with other small, protruding shapes will greatly increase air resistance. That means the car will not run as efficiently or as fast. The smart racer will pay attention to details in order to win the race.

Cost improvement is a many-lapped race, perhaps like the Indianapolis 500, but more like a sports car rally. In a rally, drivers must arrive at designated checkpoints at certain times. Winners are those racers who most closely follow the rally's instructions. Not only does this mean pinpoint timing, but accurate routing. The same can apply to a company on the course of cost improvement. Your navigator, or financial analyst, can help you stay on route so that you will arrive on time at checkpoints. Some of these checkpoints, which we will describe below, are Accounts Payable, Inventory Control, the use of Buyer/Planners, and the Make/Buy Decision.

Financial Checkpoints

Accounts Payable

The first area we will discuss is Accounts Payable. Connecting JIT delivery to JIT payment not only improves supplier relations, but eliminates much paperwork for Finance. You must stress this double-sided benefit. Of course, this is not possible until you can convince Finance to eliminate invoices for every shipment, especially if they are daily. Finance may look at your JIT payment schedule and see not less paperwork, but decidedly more. But, you can eliminate matching invoices because you have guaranteed daily shipment of quality parts through your certification program. You will soon know if a shipment was received. Your production line will not shut down. You don't need an invoice to tell you that.

Now if that sounds like a frightening way to have financial accountability, don't panic. Remember, you have built a bridge of trust with your suppliers. You have checked their financial status, their delivery reliability, their quality and you have monitored each of these areas. You have created a strong structure which will eliminate wasteful paperwork by working with Finance. You can strengthen this bridge of trust even more by paying suppliers more quickly.

Daily payment is, of course, an ideal (which, incidentally, can be greatly helped along by bar coding and EDI). But daily payment is not the only solution. If the typical wait for payment is 60 days, reward good suppliers by cutting it to 30 days; if it's 30, cut it to 15. The point is that nobody in their right mind wants to jeopardize a win/win situation. And everybody, we should add, must understand that we are looking at Accounts Payable from a total cost approach. If you lose a month of interest because you paid more quickly, then consider how much more money will be saved by eliminating unnecessary paperwork. And if that is not enough to convince Finance, ask them what is the value of having a contented supplier who delivers quality products with unswerving regularity.

Inventory Control

Accountability also becomes an area of concern for Finance in inventory control. How is it possible to track inventory in a system where work orders have been banished in favor of a pull system of manufacturing? This is one of the most prevalent excuses brought up as a reason not to adopt JIT. In a recent issue of the *Harvard Business Review*, this issue is raised and addressed in a very simple manner, one with which we wholeheartedly agree:

> "If production is simplified ... the tools required to monitor and control it can also be simplified." **(2)**

If there is little or no excess purchased inventory or finished goods inventory as is true in a JIT environment using a pull system, then the only place Finance has to check is work-in-process inventory. WIP inventory, of course, reflects actual demand placed on resources which could be generated by an MRP system based on accurate Bills of Material. Low levels of inventory are possible because company operations, including those on the production line, are balanced, thus minimizing the existence of queues. As the article says in summation, "accountants and schedulers actually have more control than in a traditional system." **(3)**

Buyer/Planners

Using buyer/planners is another tool which aids the improvement process. Buyer/planners can actually make it easier to check buying performance and to trace the money trail. All Finance has to do is ask whether or not the buyer/planner purchased the proper requirements generated by MRP (Material Requirements Planning). We have been touching on the issue of performance measurements all through this discussion. Here, we will just remind you that the responsibility and authority granted to the buyer/planner has the added advantage of allowing Finance more insight, but with no added work. Accountability is built into the system.

The Make/Purchase Decision

The Make/Buy decision may be the most important activity in which Finance and Purchasing collaborates. Purchasing has all the vital information pertaining to suppliers while Finance knows how much can be spent and how costs will be allocated. In a traditional company, these functions are distinct to each department, but in a JIT company, we have seen that the boundaries are intentionally blurred. This is particularly true for a company now using a Financial Analyst in the procurement area. Our point is that this makes the decision an easier one; the questions to be asked remain the same whether a company is traditional or not, but the company employing JIT Purchasing already has in place a system that can answer these questions. Indeed, it answers these questions constantly in its everyday operations.

Purchasing, as an evaluator of suppliers, is well equipped to rate its own company as a potential manufacturer of a part normally bought from an outside supplier. Conversely, Purchasing in consultation with Manufacturing Engineering can recommend that its company stop manufacturing a part and buy it from an outside supplier instead. The watchwords here, as in all procurement decisions, are quality, deliverability and total cost. The decision of whether to make or buy ultimately depends upon how to utilize the company resources. When reduced to its simplest terms, the Make/Buy decision is clearly a responsibility divided equally between Purchasing and Finance.

We should not say "divided." A better word is "shared," as in sharing information. Purchasing has the cost and capacity figures for outside suppliers. It has a certification program in place which it can also use to evaluate its own company. Finance has programs and systems to ascertain the most profitable use of resources. The two functions fit so well together that it is a surprise to us that more companies do not make objective make/buy studies.

There are other factors besides cost and production capacity to take into consideration, as pointed out in the following table:

Make/Purchase Decisions

Considerations for Make
  Cost vs. price considerations
  Integrating supplier and plant objectives
  Plant capacity issues
  Confidentiality of design
  Supplier capability lacking
Considerations for Purchase
  Suppliers' research and development
  Cost vs. price considerations
  Volume and delivery requirements
  Production capability
  Subcontracting
  Multiple-source vs. single-source vs. sole-source policy

Company decisions are, of course, dictated by market conditions. Indeed, all financial plans are formulated with an eye on the domestic and international economy. Although we won't give a primer on economics, we will demonstrate how JIT Purchasing can enhance your ability to weather the storms and lulls of business cycles.

Market Conditions

All business philosophies, including JIT, are subject to the laws of supply and demand. All seek to find the equilibrium where supply and demand curves cross.

JIT Purchasing, however, is far more flexible than other approaches. With its concern for total costs, it is not as subject to the whims of economic conditions. For example, a JIT buyer is under no pressure to purchase parts because market conditions have substantially lowered their price. There may be an immediate savings, but it will quickly disappear when quality and inventory carrying costs are added in. Also, what would happen if this buyer bought 10,000 electric motors of a certain size and Design and Marketing decide they will now build the product with smaller motors? That company is stuck with motors it can't use and for which it still has to pay.

All of us, we are sure, have had a grandmother who would give the following advice: "It isn't a bargain if you don't need it." Grandma was right! This is what we mean, by the way, when we say that JIT revisits traditional practices. Waste, in earlier times in our country's history, was abhorrent. As economic conditions changed and resources became abundant, we started to forget the old advice. Now, we find ourselves with companies which were organized to take advantage of our vast resources and our dominant position in the world market.

Those times no longer exist. That is not to say that we have returned to earlier times either. Where we are is in a highly, interdependent international economy. It calls for a whole new strategy in which long-range financial goals dictate short-term policies, instead of the other way around.

Let's go back to the buyer we were discussing above. She no longer procures material based on price alone. She is also a planner who is aware of her company's long-range goals and the needs of the company as a whole. She and her partners have developed a supplier certification program which makes suppliers part of a team working toward a common goal as well. She makes frequent, small purchases because she can rely on these suppliers to deliver good quality parts on a pinpoint schedule. When she finds that the prices of certain parts are higher because of certain market conditions, she does not panic. She knows that, in the long run, higher prices will be offset by lower prices caused by more favorable market conditions.

In short, JIT Purchasing smooths out the fluctuations inherent in any economy by emphasizing total cost and by working with a "pull" system of production which include suppliers who have reduced costs and lead-times. Since JIT Purchasing also emphasizes planning, buyer/planners are trained to look at the effects of market conditions and forecasts when researching sources and procuring material. It is this mind-set which will help the most to bring Finance into the present and then into the future. Future costs are just as important in purchasing decisions as present conditions and past histories.

Legal Issues and Ethics

The last area to cover in this chapter on Finance has to do with legal issues and ethics. Since there are legal implications to pricing, let's broadly review the antitrust laws.

SHERMAN ANTITRUST ACT: Passed by Congress in 1890. It prohibits contracts, conspiracies, or combinations which act in restraint of trade or attempt to monopolize any part of interstate trade. Business firms can not lawfully make price agreements that restrain trade except where they are exempted or where they do not affect interstate commerce.

CLAYTON ACT: Passed in 1914. It prohibits price discrimination between different buyers where the effect is substantially to lessen competition or tend to create a monopoly in any line of business.

FEDERAL TRADE COMMISSION ACT: Passed in 1914. The FTC is given the power to issue "cease and desist" orders against parties not abiding by the acts and subsequent interpretation by the courts.

ROBINSON PATMAN ACT: Passed in 1936. This act makes it unlawful for sellers to discriminate in price between buyers of like grade and quality materials where the consequence of so doing tends to create a monopoly or to injure, destroy, or prevent competition. It also prevents sellers from offering brokerage fees to buyers except for services actually rendered to the seller. Sellers can not pay for advertising and similar services unless they are made available on proportionally equal terms to all buyers.

Purchasing's role in the JIT environment is to consider price as one variable in determining whether to buy material. The laws stated above do not prohibit Purchasing Departments from buying from sellers with higher prices. Although our advice should not be construed with a lawyer's, we believe that as long as you stress that quality and delivery are factors in considering whether to purchase or not and you give all sellers equal opportunity and information, you will not run afoul of the law.

Our discussion here focused on antitrust laws. We would also remind you of the Uniform Commercial Code (UCC) which also applies in all states except Louisiana. Basically, the UCC says that past performance dictates future action.

Ethics often supercedes the law and our advice here is quite direct and simple: Don't violate these laws and don't get involved with companies who do. We must remain ethical in all our business dealings, not only because it is morally right (and that *is* most important), but because it is simply good business. Circumventing the law or moral practices invites disaster because it introduces variables over which we no longer have any control.

Unethical behavior also destroys any bridges of trust which you have built between your company and the outside world. Without those bridges, you won't be able to do your job with any degree of efficiency.

We have one last word on the Purchasing/Finance interface. We have emphasized the need for Finance and Purchasing to build bridges in order to make better-informed decisions. Because we mention only these two departments in this chapter does not mean they are the only two departments who should be involved. It is obvious that this decision can be greatly aided by input from Engineering, Production, Quality, etc. Purchasing is in a unique position to facilitate the formation of a team approach to problem-solving in a company. Before we discuss the Purchasing Team, however, there are still more bridges to build before we sleep, to paraphrase Robert Frost. The next one is with the Manufacturing area of your company and your suppliers.

CHAPTER SEVEN: Planning: Challenge and Opportunity

We have arrived at an important destination along the route to JIT. All the bridges we have built, like the arteries of your body, terminate here at the heart of your company — Manufacturing. You are not in business to implement new philosophies; you are in business to make a profit by manufacturing a product. All too often, this obvious point is missed. Neglect the heart at the peril of ceasing to be.

It is not enough for Purchasing to make sure that Manufacturing receives a healthy diet of materials to supply its production line. Purchasing also has the responsibility to coordinate shipments of quality goods with production schedules, preventive maintenance, service and the acquisition of capital equipment.

With respect to Manufacturing, Purchasing should think of itself as a sports doctor who helps an athlete perform at peak levels. In short, Purchasing's job is to help Manufacturing excel according to a regimen of precise deliveries of quality parts with no waste, scrap or rework.

Manufacturing Resource Planning (MRP II) will link Purchasing and Manufacturing. Like many management tools, MRP II is misunderstood. Some confuse it with Material Requirements Planning (MRP I); others with an inventory control system or a production control system.

Overall, MRP II is a method to manage the business, not just parts of it. Its successful implementation begins at the highest level in the organization and does not stop until everyone and everything is managed and directed. Although this may sound rigid, the fact is that an MRP II structure is adaptable to change.

Previously, we hinted at how this adaptability can grow out of a structure centered around function. We gave the example of the Buyer/Planner, pointing out that such an employee was in the best position to work with suppliers. Why was this true? Because, the employee who is part of a buying and planning team does not get news second hand about the changing manufacturing environment. That person not only watches change develop; he participates in its development. Thus, he has a far better understanding of the manufacturing environment in the plant. This translates into better purchasing decisions as well as improved supplier relations.

Out of this certainty that there would be change, MRP II was developed.

The Evolving Role of Purchasing and MRP II

Companies make forecasts and set schedules based on these forecasts. As actual sales materialize, a discrepancy develops between the forecasted and the actual. This varying demand causes some products to move ahead of schedule and some to be delayed or cancelled entirely. Forecasts are developed from the best information available at the time. But, after the forecast is made, things begin to happen — emergency breakdowns, unexpected shortages, and demand changes. Internally, we face engineering changes, material substitutions, late deliveries, scrap, rework, inventory errors, quality and tooling problems, inoperative machines, absenteeism, paperwork errors and changes in the delivery schedule.

In other words, a lot can and will happen. Every one of these changes in a production plan also means supplier activities must change. But, we must move away from the reactive end of the spectrum to the proactive end. The ability of an organization to manage change is the key to success and the need for this ability manifests itself more and more as the organization grows. Most manual systems cannot cope with the constant changes. Consequently, the organization finds itself in the middle of an ever more confusing state where due dates are not met and where there is more work-in-process, raw material and finished inventory than necessary. With the confusion comes frustration, since people want to do their jobs well but are unable because there is no organized structure.

Computers today have the power, speed and capacity to manipulate massive amounts of data. Of course, if we use them merely to speed up a questionable process, we will only obtain chaos faster. Clearly, there are intervening steps between manual systems and computers.

The best way for Purchasing to view MRP II is to see it as an evolutionary process. MRP is a computerized system in which bills of material are exploded and collated to come up with a precise, real-time picture of material needs. Upon this foundation, or from this simpler form of animal, evolves MRP II which coordinates the resources of Manufacturing and suppliers. However, you can't allocate resources to manufacture products if there is no material. Hence, MRP II is also known as a "closed loop system" and evolved through the following steps:

THE EVOLUTION OF MRP II

1. An Organized Ordering Method — Projection/Backlog of Demand
2. Reorder Point/EOQ
3. Priority Planning — Development of a Master Plan
4. Material Requirements Planning (MRP) — Determination of Purchasing and Manufacturing Requirements
5. Manufacturing Resource Planning (MRP II) — Communication of Needs to Resources and Service Agencies

Purchasing has already begun to undergo a similar evolution, but it still has a way to go before it will catch up with MRP II and use it to the best advantage as we will discuss below. Presently, MRP II generates the following elements:

THE ELEMENTS OF MRP II

BUSINESS PLANNING
SALES PLANNING
PRODUCTION PLANNING
MASTER PRODUCTION SCHEDULING
MATERIALS PLANNING
CAPACITY PLANNING
PURCHASING
SHOP FLOOR CONTROL
PERFORMANCE MEASUREMENTS

These elements are generated according to the following flow chart:

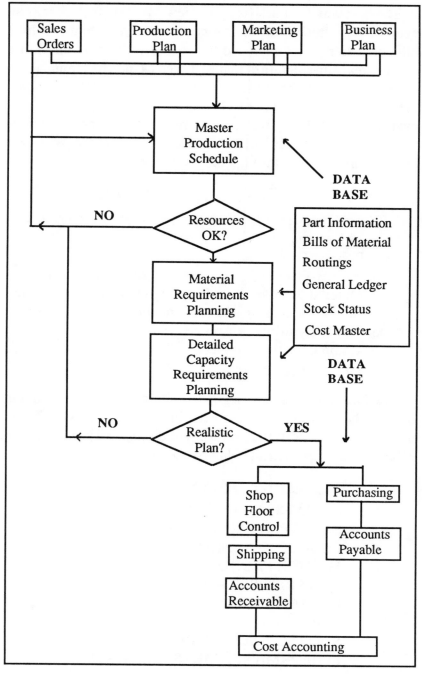

The MRP II information is then passed on to a planner who then alerts a buyer to purchase the required material from suppliers. In JIT Purchasing, one step is eliminated. Now, the information from MRP II is handed over to a Buyer/Planner who is responsible for both functions. In the future, we would like to see this process collapse even further. In the next stage of the evolution of JIT Purchasing, operators, foremen and receiving personnel would release the information, based on 100% accurate Bills of Material, directly to the supplier. This would free Purchasing to be responsible for negotiating terms and conditions and long-term agreements.

As we shall see, MRP II is a logical approach to business which takes the chaos out and puts organization and control in the hands of employees at all levels of the organization. We must remember that MRP II is a planning tool utilizing computers, not a replacement for employees. It is also a tool with many elements which require teamwork. Let's take a look at the Manufacturing elements above and see how they relate to Purchasing.

Business Planning

MRP II provides an organization with answers to questions arising in the planning process. Many people mistakenly believe this process begins with the forecast. It does not: it begins with top management. Top management provides leadership to the organization not only in financial and motivational areas, but, most importantly, in setting and then constantly emphasizing the overall direction of the company.

By assuming this leadership role, top management engages in the following activities:

- Setting overall objectives for the organization
- Establishing responsibility
- Managing the business plan
- Insuring execution of the plan
- Measuring performance

In setting objectives, the system/software capacity is invaluable in constructing and running "what if" models. In such a model, MRP II furnishes management with possible action plans given the current status of inventory, production capacity and manpower. From these hypothetical situations, top management can then choose the direction which insures proper growth while maintaining profitability.

Once the primary objectives are chosen, each department within the company assumes the responsibility of initiating and carrying out plans supporting the company's overall direction. Management then oversees the individual plans and determines whether they conform or deviate from the overall course.

Sales Planning

Once objectives are set, forecasts drive much of the planning process even when actual orders take priority. The primary reason for sales planning is to provide information to Manufacturing on how the business plan will be met. It also provides a vehicle to determine capacity, manpower and inventory needs as well as helping the organization work more closely together. The sales plan acts as a guide from which management determines how to best use its resources.

Notice that we are moving closer and closer to a philosophy in which no department initiates an action without consultation with other departments. As the forecast becomes reality in the form of customer orders, Sales and Manufacturing must meet often and review discrepancies in order to make adjustments. They must also meet with Purchasing because, in a JIT environment, it is actual orders which "pull" products from suppliers to manucturers to customers. And, of course, it is Purchasing's job to supply the line with the necessary material. In such a balanced system, constant communication is not a luxury; it is a necessity.

Production Planning

At this stage in MRP II, we are still using a wide-angle lens to view the manufacturing landscape, rather than a telephoto lens.

Zooming in on specifics, such as availability of specific parts, would be difficult to accomplish based solely on the business plan, sales plan and forecasts. Production planning, therefore, surveys availability and capacities in three broad areas:

- Manpower
- Equipment
- Material (Make or Purchase)

This approach also extends to time. The production and procurement plan, although broken down into monthly or weekly intervals, covers a one- to two-year horizon. During this period, the plan becomes a regulator or measuring stick, allowing the buyer/planner to define the amount of inventory via the production rate. The amount of inventory to be manufactured or purchased is then checked against the estimates of the production plan on a monthly or weekly schedule.

Like other facets of MRP II, production planning allows both manufacturing and supplier management to test choices based on the limits or possibilities dictated by the three broad areas mentioned above. Within these parameters, MRP II aids management in charting a course which will support the sales plan. No company's purchasing department can expect to control inventory without a well-managed production plan.

Production planning and purchasing act, in fact, as a warning system. It provides management with a tool to control equipment, manpower and material. Previously unseen problems come into focus, moving management to a decision point.

On our flow chart on page 106, we see this point as a question: Do we have the capacity to perform to the production plan? If the answer is "no," we must loop back to either the sales or business plan. If we don't have adequate resources or can't procure them, we must revise the sales plan.

Revising the plan, of course, is not our only alternative. We can, as noted above, add to the staff, use subcontractors, purchase more equipment to improve our capacity. How can Purchasing assist in the process of procuring capital equipment?

There are two major reasons why Purchasing should assist. One, Purchasing knows the suppliers. Buyers are trained to collect information and to find favorable buying conditions. Two, Purchasing is the depository of information about internal company operations in a JIT environment. As such, it is best equipped to coordinate the varying needs of all departments.

In its first capacity, Purchasing gets the information needed by the user of the equipment from various manufacturers. The user's department then studies the specifications and capabilities of the machinery to determine whether it will meet their requirements. At this point, Purchasing's second role comes into play. Other departments are brought in to discuss the impact this purchase will have on their departments as well as to provide input about adjustments or alternatives which may result. We have already discussed how this team approach works in the chapters on Quality and Engineering Design. Again, the hypothesis-checking of MRP II acts as a model for team discussion.

Another important input will come from the Maintenance department. The following is a checklist to use when procuring capital equipment:

- Will the equipment require special maintenance procedures or personnel?
- Will the equipment operate at least to minimum requirements?
- Will we have trouble locating spare parts? Are they expensive? Must they be special-ordered?
- Will we need any special training in maintenance procedures and, if so, who will train our personnel?
- Will there be a need for special testing equipment? What percentage of faults will standard procedures detect?
- Will we need to establish special safety procedures?

Obviously, these questions have a major bearing on cost. These are the types of questions Purchasing must ask. They may not be apparent to the equipment user. In addition, Purchasing is better equipped to negotiate and, perhaps most importantly, knows or can seek the reliability of suppliers. We are all aware of the disastrous effects of bargains that come in the back door because somebody thought they found a real good deal. Perhaps the most important lesson of is that procurements and plans which can't stand the heat of team questioning are best left out.

Master Scheduling

Let's go back to the MRP II flow chart. We have passed through a decision point and have determined that the resources are in place to support the production plan. It is now time to begin the Material Requirement Planning (MRP) phase. First, we encounter the master schedule which specifically determines what will be produced and when. It must be a realistic schedule, that is, a schedule which is "doable" by Manufacturing.

To begin, Purchasing must help pull together the following data in order to employ MRP — Bills of Material, Shop Routings, Engineering Change Orders and Inventory.

Bills of Material

Bills of material accurately list the items used in producing a finished good and the level at which each item is added to the assembly. You can compare a bill to a recipe which lists the ingredients and in what proportions to blend them into the dish you are making. Surprisingly enough, it is common for companies to produce finished goods from inaccurate bills. Some companies use no bills of material at all. The latter case may work for the "cook" who throws a plastic pouch in boiling water, but not for the "chef" who must prepare more elaborate concoctions.

Just as the chef must prepare an accurate list of ingredients needed to make a complicated meal, so must Purchasing insist on a 100% accurate bill of materials. Incorrect bills lead to faulty planning and execution of the production plan. For example, if a bill lists a component not used in producing a product, either inventory will grow or someone must intervene and cancel an order for that component. If that person forgets or goes on vacation, unnecessary inventory will be procured and stored. Conversely, if a bill does not list a required component, either the finished product will be incorrect or a "catch-up shortage" environment will be created. In either example, it is far easier to maintain an accurate bill of material which negates the need for special handling. The application of MRP will result in frustration if your bills are incorrect.

Shop Routings

Shop routings are the basic plan for the manufacturing of a particular item. They answer three questions:

1. Where are the items produced?
2. What must be done to produce the items and with what tools?
3. How long does it take to produce the items?

Usually, there is a primary and alternate routing. Alternate routings come into use when capacity overages or machine breakdowns occur. Primary routings are the most efficient and least costly. Routings can also involve subcontractors. Here, Purchasing has the responsibility of making sure this information is current. Purchasing also has responsibility for seeing that routings are under control in a supplier's plant.

Engineering Change Orders

Engineering change orders (ECOs) are another key element in the management of an MRP system. Clearly, an engineering change affects the bill of material and, as we have seen, that will eventually affect inventory as obsolescence and scrap. All these changes have a direct bearing on the domain of Purchasing — product cost and procurement. Purchasing's goal is to allow for these changes while maintaining an accurate bill of materials. Achieving that goal is both easy and hard; easy, if you do it and very hard, if you don't. There are two rules to follow for ECOs:

1. Identify the timing of the ECO implementation.
2. Notify all areas affected by the change.

We have found that the best way to follow these rules is to make one person responsible for the bills and their accuracy. That person must be notified of all changes to the bill. He or she must then alert all affected departments such as Purchasing in the case of a purchased part change. Others should be notified as required by your company's definition of functional responsibility. The point we wish to make is that shared information not only promotes accuracy, but breaks down departmental walls.

Imagine yourself racing a 12-meter yacht. You better let your crew know if you are putting up a new sail or changing your tack. If you don't, you may find that you have left some of your crew behind. Yacht racing is a precision sport. Maneuvers happen so suddenly that unprepared crew members can be literally swept off the decks. The manufacturing plant operates as close to precision as possible, too. If you fail to notify a segment of your organization of a change, you may find yourself sailing back to retrieve a department swept overboard by an unannounced change.

Inventory Control and Record Accuracy

As we have repeatedly seen, the master production schedule and, indeed, all of MRP II thrives on accuracy which is only difficult to achieve if you fail to strive for it. Here, too, we advocate making one person responsible for maintaining the item master and accountable for insuring the accuracy of its data. This is as true for a supplier's plant as it is for your own company. In fact, accuracy of data is the key to credibility with suppliers. The less changes there are, the more predictability.

Once material has been identified by type — raw material, work-in-process, and finished goods — and by storage location, inventory management becomes easier as the computer stores information which is both timely and accurate. Of course, we must still guard against GIGO — garbage in, garbage out. In Chapter 3, we discussed cycle-counting as one way to determine

whether files were accurate. In cycle-counting, you will remember, physical counting is combined with auditing in order not only to locate inaccuracies, but to locate the sources of inaccuracies. Once that is done, problem solving techniques are employed to eliminate the cause of the inaccuracy.

When it comes to inventory, record accuracy is the issue needing attention. Whether your store rooms are closed, open or limited has an effect on MRP, but training and educating employees in record accuracy is the primary focus. Store room employees must know procedures which insure accuracy and require follow-up audits. In JIT, solving a problem does not mean locating and then treating only the symptoms.

Lastly, we mention quality's role in the relationship between MRP and inventory. The inventory record compiled for MRP assumes all inventory is good. Some method of quality control should be evaluated and implemented so that available inventory which is listed in MRP is, in fact, free of defects.

Another quality issue centers around the Material Review Boards. Although not strictly a requirement of MRP, some companies have found them to be effective in dealing with rejected raw material, work-in-process material or finished goods. We tend to agree given certain conditions. Typically, Material Review Boards only deal with symptoms in that they determine whether parts can be used "as is," reworked or scrapped. Our view is that this is not enough. Like the audit phase of cycle-counting, review boards should also be responsible for determining the source of the reject and then solving the problem so that it will not occur again. The ultimate goal of a review board is to put itself out of business by solving the causes of rejects.

Materials Planning

At last, we move down the flow chart to material planning. What we have discussed under the heading of the master production schedule are the ingredients — inventory, bills of material, etc. — used in the MRP recipe. These ingredients are mixed in the computer and out comes a material plan. MRP, then, is the set of instructions used to "bake" this plan. We might add that the ingredients had better be accurate or you will end up with a "half-baked" plan.

The instructions of MRP form a straight-forward series of steps. They are:

1. Explode the bills of material from the net master production schedule to determine the MRP gross requirement for its components.
2. Net the on-hand inventory balance against the gross requirement.
3. Look for any open orders which can be rescheduled to meet demand (both purchase and work orders).
4. Recommend an order quantity using lot size and lead time information.

In the execution of MRP, the computer begins with the top level of a particular bill of material and moves down through the other levels to determine if the inventory exists or if it needs to be procured. The power of this system rests in the computer's ability to manipulate massive amounts of data in a quick and accurate manner. This manipulation of data determines what material is needed at various stages in the manufacturing process and when it should be purchased. Most MRP systems today also allow for the allocation of inventory which exists in the store room, but have been promised to an order. In short, MRP allows manufacturers to control a process which is subject to frequent changes in orders, inventory records and bills of material.

In the last step, MRP determines order quantities. We have already discussed lot size and economic order quantities in Chapter 1, so let's concentrate here on lead time which is of utmost importance to Purchasing. Lead-time accuracy is just as critical here as in any other facet of MRP II. This is because the computer will either launch or recommend that orders be launched based on the lead time identified for both purchased and manufactured items.

Lead time breaks down into 5 components:

Queue — time material is staged ahead of a work center waiting for its turn to be set up and run.

Set-up — process of getting the machine ready to run the part.

Run — time actually spent processing parts at a work center.

Wait — time the parts sit after processing and before being moved to the next work center.

Move — time spent moving parts to the next work center whereupon the parts enter a queue again.

In our experience, we have found that over half of the lead time is taken up by queues. This is important to note because Purchasing has the capability in a JIT plant of greatly reducing queue time by having material from suppliers shipped directly to the point on the production line where it is needed, when it is needed. Here, we see a clear example of how Purchasing activities directly affect Manufacturing operations. Shorter lead times mean that inventory turns over faster, resulting in a greater return on assets, while still providing Manufacturing with an uninterrupted supply of material.

Capacity Planning

Capacity planning looks at the shop schedule (released shop orders and planned order release which have just been generated) and uses the routing file to determine the number of hours required at each work center. Unlike the rough cut capacity plan done by production planning, this capacity plan identifies every work center and every operation required to meet the master production schedule. The decision point we face here is: "Do we have the capacity to carry out the schedule?" If not, then we need to consider alternatives — overtime, additional shifts, alternate routings, outside contracting, adding resources (people or equipment). If the answer is affirmative, MRP II flows down the chart to Purchasing.

Purchasing

With respect to MRP II, Purchasing has the responsibility of contracting with suppliers for the purchase of materials, goods and services to meet the requirements of the master production schedule. While the MRP system generates the requirements, Purchasing may override quantities after carefully considering total costs. Quantity discounts, systems contracts and stocking arrangements all figure in the decision.

Suppliers' performance, as we have noted before, also figures heavily into the purchasing equation. Many times, the ability of a supplier to perform is dependent upon the speed at which they are notified of a need or a change in a need. This is where the buyer/planner we discussed in Chapter 2 fits in. In MRP II, it is common for an inventory planner to receive the requirement report from MRP for purchased materials. The inventory planner evaluates the recommendation and passes the requisition on to Purchasing which then places the orders. With a buyer/planner, however, the need for somebody to review the information between the computer generation and Purchasing is eliminated.

Shop Floor Control

Shop Floor Control is the management of material flowing through the plant. It begins with facilities planning, which not only deals with capital investments, but with the placement of equipment. Along with input from industrial engineers, plant management seeks to improve and control work-in-process flow. Once material and work orders (based on MRP requirements) have been issued to the floor, manufacturing begins. As work progresses from work center to work center, most MRP systems have the ability to track each operation. The master scheduler can then monitor the progress of the material.

Backlogs, productivity variances, machine downtime, scrap and rejects all contribute to the problems the scheduler and shop supervision must respond to. In order for MRP to be effective, we must insure due date integrity for each operation. Any time we miss a date in this process, we must analyze the structure for corrective action.

First line supervision, thus, has the responsibility to execute the shop schedule generated by MRP. This includes the due date as well as balancing the line and flow of material. Since plans generated by MRP can only be fulfilled if materials are available on time, supervisors must perceive themselves as executors and not victims of the plans. First line supervisors are the leaders on the shop floor and need the authority and responsibility to carry out the plan. Thus, they should receive realistic schedules as poorly planned ones will dilute their ability to properly execute the shop schedule.

Reporting

Reporting for an MRP system depends on feedback which assists managers in their particular areas. Some systems have instantaneous reporting via a terminal and by hard copy, while others only have hard copy reports. However the information is relayed, the purpose of reporting is to evaluate the performance of the plant in meeting its objectives. Since our primary objective is to meet the needs of the customer, all reporting must keep that in mind.

Summary reporting provides management with the means to be in control without wading through reams of paper documents. Exception reporting, of course, deals with the significant element being measured. Together, they are a highly valuable tool for management, but a tool that must be managed as well. Reports must be on time and unnecessary reports must not be generated. This requires constant evaluation of the available reports. Finally, an MRP system should be flexible enough for you to generate customized reports which pertain to your company's individual needs. The following is a listing of some typical MRP reports:

FORECAST AND DEMAND SUMMARY REPORT — Compares actual demand to sales order forecast. Report is sequenced by part number and order type; can be printed for all, selected, or a range of part numbers.

MASTER PRODUCTION SCHEDULE REPORT — Prints a report of the Master Production Schedule for all part numbers, selected part numbers, or a range of part numbers. Options include creating different level reports and updating of Master Schedule Files for use with Rough Cut Capacity Planning, Detail Capacity Planning and Requirements Planning.

SUMMARIZED ROUGH CUT REQUIREMENTS — Prints for each designated time period and work center, the required load, the over/under load, and the percent load. Information is also accumulated and cumulative data are printed.

SUPPLIER ANALYSIS REPORT — Shows delivery performance on all purchase orders for selected suppliers. Calculates average days late and reject rate.

CONSOLIDATED REQUIREMENTS — Reports on a part's gross and net requirements and detail information concerning open purchase orders, work orders, schedules, and pegging.

RETURN ON ASSETS — Describes utilization of total assets available to company with respect to material, manpower, equipment and productivity.

DETAIL CAPACITY REQUIREMENTS — Projects machine and labor capacity requirements by resource and period. Required capacity is compared to available capacity and the percent load is calculated. Past due orders are also flagged.

PERFORMANCE TO SCHEDULE — Provides variances between actual factory performance and planned schedule.

SHIPPING COMMITMENT — Prints report showing part shipping commitments for the next six months.

Summary

As with any system, MRP II and MRP are only tools for getting our job done. Management must review all the generated information and make judgements which are best for the organization. At no time should anybody assume that the information is sacrosanct. You should always have the power to override the recommended orders the system developed. Remember: MRP II is not just a computer system, it is a method of operating and managing your company. It is the bridge between Purchasing, Manufacturing and the Customer.

CHAPTER EIGHT: Auditing and Performance Measurements

We measure performance in order to be predictable, so that we know where we have been, where we are and where we are going. In short, so we don't make the same mistake twice. Of course, it is possible to measure the wrong items, to measure after the fact and to measure meaningless quantities. The problem with the old yardsticks of performance measurements is that they are guilty of these misrepresentations of actual sales, forecasts, schedules and productivity because they use a reactive, rather than a proactive scale.

Today's Purchasing Managers must use new yardsticks which collect data and look at it over a period of time. Thus, when we make decisions, we will be able to compare actual data against predicted performance. This gives us the opportunity to take corrective action. This is what we mean to be proactive: to measure the predictability of the outcomes of decision-making.

A Purchasing Manager cannot wait for problems. He or she must review what the plant community needs and communicate those desires to the supplier base in a manner which avoids expediting, firefighting and other wasteful activities. In addition, Purchasing must be aware of both manufacturing and marketing requirements in order to satisfy customers' demands. In order to be on top of the situation, accurate information is a necessity.

Accuracy is best obtained through a system of measurement that reflects a Total Business Concept because this is what JIT/TQC is based upon. We will discuss these new TBC yardsticks in this chapter — what they measure and why. For now, let's look at their general characteristics.

In general, the use of TBC measurements by Purchasing will show:

1. How close we are to having on-line, real-time information about both internal and external Manufacturing operations as well as Purchasing activities. Current information coupled with a documented past is useful information.

2. How accurate our information is. We all know that a small mistake compounds over time. Unlike interest on your personal investments, this is not favorable. The surveyor who makes a mistake of one degree can cost you many valuable acres of land.

3. How much waste is present in Manufacturing operations and Purchasing activities. Waste, today, is too often accepted as a given and absorbed into overhead costs. This is truly a reactive way of thinking and must change as we compete in a world market.

4. How actual performance compares to the stated plan. Observing this variance is instrumental in making new plans which take corrective action. Those who don't learn from the mistakes of the past are doomed to repeat them.

Purchasing has a unique opportunity and obligation to initiate TBC measurements, but it cannot succeed alone. Previously, we showed how Purchasing will work with Finance in the establishment of new yardsticks based on total cost. This relationship must continue in the area of performance measurement as well. Certainly, Engineering, Quality and Manufacturing have a large role to play, too. Purchasing must not think its responsibility begins with a request to buy and ends when the material reaches the receiving room door. Keep in mind what we said back in the first two chapters about the changing role of Purchasing which is better defined as Procurement and Materials Management. Purchasing's responsibility begins with the birth of an idea for a new product, follows it through its development in Design, its future plans in marketing, its construction in Manufacturing and its eventual "leaving of the nest" in Sales and ends once any field failures are resolved. Keeping track of the product's maturation is why Purchasing measure performance.

Another responsibility of Purchasing while measuring performance is to monitor the progress of implementing JIT/TQC. In essence, this is the same as measuring the performance of the whole company.

Purchasing's last, but not least, responsibility is to measure its own performance. This does not mean only measuring the performance of the buyer or the ability to insure on-time delivery, but also measuring how well it measures the performance of the rest of the company.

Performance measurement is a difficult job which, because of the relative importance of purchased material, makes it all the more critical for Purchasing to lead the company. But, as we stated above, it cannot be done alone. Thomas Peters in his book, *Thriving on Chaos,* states that today we need flexibility every bit as much as we need excellence. American business people and decision makers must be shaken up. "What is needed, he insists, is intelligence, energy, heroic efforts and a renewed emphasis on quality products and performance." (**1**) This is what teamwork is all about — getting people to appraise your performance so you can see if the outcome you predicted coincides with the state of the real world.

We divide performance measurement into three areas — financial measurement, self-measurement by Purchasing and operational measurements. Let's briefly review what we said earlier about the first area.

We stressed the need for Purchasing and Finance to build bridges between each other, to work together in the implementation of JIT/TQC practices. The principal thrust of our discussion was to emphasize a total cost-oriented, rather than a price-oriented, approach in financial measurements. The method we advocated to pave the way for this new approach was financial analysis which attempts to gain financial control through cost improvement.

There were two principles behind cost improvement. One, we should not look at price alone in seeking to maximize profits, but also look at quality, quantity and delivery. Two, we should measure variances against cost, not price when evaluating our profitability. These two principles work in tandem with the basic principles of JIT/TQC, that is, build to demand and the elimination of excess inventory and wasteful operations. We should only incur costs, then, when material or operations add value to the product we are building. This concept is a change from the present measurement of Purchase Price Variance employed by many organizations today.

As we streamline our plant through the reduction of costs, we found that Finance's job actually became easier as accountability was built into the process of manufacturing. For example, we pointed out that Finance's accounting of inventory became easier when we eliminated safety stocks and reduced queues and lead times. In the JIT/TQC environment, inventory could be accounted for merely by looking at the levels of work-in-process. By giving up traditional manufacturing and accounting practices, we may be able to have more control than before.

The second area of performance measurement is Purchasing's measurement of its own performance. In a certain sense, of course, all the measurements of which we speak in this chapter are self-measurements. If Purchasing is doing its job right, this will be reflected in the performance of the whole company. There are, however, some measurements which pertain to Purchasing alone and particularly to the activity of buyer/planners who are becoming the backbone of many Purchasing departments.

The first set of measurements is concerned with quality, specifically the level of quality attained by your company's suppliers. An overall measurement of the success of your quality program is the number of suppliers who are participating in your Supplier Certification Program. The number of participants alone is not as important as who the suppliers are. In other words, you should have a high percentage of participants for those 25% of your suppliers that account for 90-95% of the value of your purchased material. The goal is to achieve 100% of your suppliers shipping 100% quality and delivery.

You should also be measuring how each supplier ranks in your certification program. Obviously, if you see that a supplier's quality rating is slipping, then you have a problem. We have three pertinent measurements for rating supplier's performance:

1. Supplier Quality Rating (SQR) — determined by incoming inspection

$$SQR = \frac{\text{Lots Accepted}}{\text{Lots Inspected}} \quad X \quad \frac{\text{Samples Accepted}}{\text{Samples Inspected}} \quad X \quad 100$$

2. Incoming Parts Per Million (IPPM) — determined by incoming inspection

$$IPPM = \frac{\text{Defective Samples}}{\text{Samples Inspected}} \quad X \quad 1,000,000$$

3. Manufacturing Parts Per Million (MPPM) — reported by each manufacturing area

$$MPPM = \frac{\text{Defective Parts}}{\text{Parts Used}} \quad X \quad 1,000,000$$

Of course, as TQC becomes the norm in your plant, the number of incoming inspectors should decrease correspondingly. Thus, this also becomes a good performance measurement of your quality program. Your goal is to eliminate final inspection at the supplier and at your Incoming Inspection.

The second set of measurements is more specifically concerned with buyer/planner and departmental performance. We advocate that once a year Purchasing establish cost objectives or target pricing for material purchases in the future. The degree of performance for an A item should be higher than a C item, since we place more weight on the performance of the former. Therefore, we should be asking about purchase order aging both for orders that are placed and for requisitions needing to be placed and not the number of orders placed by each buyer.

Surely, you have run across the situation where you walk into the Purchasing office and find requisitions that have been sitting there for several weeks. Establish a goal that purchase orders must be placed within 24 hours and measure your progress toward that goal. Our objective is system contracting and long-term agreements, not placing purchase orders.

In addition to the above, we suggest the following self-measurements:

> Actual vs. planned total costs and lead times
> Number of new agreements reached
> Number of single sources developed
> Number of suppliers reduced
> Number of parts consolidated
> Number of on-time deliveries per order per buyer
> Number of past due orders per supplier
> Total cost savings

Now we come to the third area of performance measurement, an area we call TBC (Total Business Concept) measurements because they measure the performance of the total company. There are many of them. To help in this area, we have developed an audit procedure to assess the JIT/TQC capabilities of your operations. There are, of course, no right or wrong answers. The point of this audit is to show that there is always room for improvement. Also, these measurements apply to suppliers as well. Purchasing should help them in setting up monitoring procedures.

The JIT/TQC Purchasing Audit

Throughput

What percentage of your total purchased inventory has been sold? _____%

Throughput measures the total amount of production which has been sold. If you bought enough material and components to build 100 products, built 80, have enough material to build 20 more in queue, and stored 10 units in finished goods inventory, your throughput percentage is 70%. Traditional methods would not detect the 30 units either in production or waiting to be sold. They may indicate that the throughput level is at 80 or even 100%, since there is no material left in the storeroom. But, a TBC measurement makes no distinctions (as far as the bottom line goes) between material in a queue or in finished goods. The criteria here is simply how much did you sell. If you are overproducing, this measurement tells you so. It may indicate that you are not building to demand, that your company is still operating in a "push," rather than a "pull," environment.

Reduced Set-Up Times

By what percentage have your suppliers and plant reduced set-up times? _____%

Set-up time is the amount of time it takes to change over a work center from the production of one item to another item. It is measured from the point where the last good product was produced for item #1 to the first good product of item #2. Set-up time is one of the first areas to attack in reducing lead times. It is also a highly visible area which can act as a great motivator to the implementation of further JIT practices. For example, we have a client who was able to reduce one set-up time from 35 minutes to 9 seconds. Broadcasting that reduction around the plant only served to make people want to reduce the set-up times at their work centers by similar percentages.

It is quite evident that reduced set-up times increase the production rate and subsequently lower inventory levels. Another equally valid result is the ability now for production lines to be much more flexible and to reduce lot sizes. This, in turn, allows you to come closer and closer to building products based on actual demand without storing excess inventory.

Ship-to-Stock vs. Ship-to-WIP

What percentage of your procured material is shipped directly to Work-In-Process? _____% To stock? ___%

This measurement presupposes that you first have on-time delivery to your receiving area. If you do not, refer to the next measurement described. Since the intent of JIT Purchasing is to get the right material to the right place at the right time so that any procedure or operation adds value to the product, it is clear that you should want to lower the percentage of material which is stored in the stockroom. Material delivered to WIP is ready to be worked upon; it does not sit in storage or queues adding carrying costs to your bottom line. Supplier Certification will contribute to achievements in this area.

Lead Time

What percentage of material is actually being processed as opposed to sitting in queue? ___% Describe your work center queues: Nonexistent __ Low (minutes) __ Moderate (hours) __ High (days) __ Very High (weeks) __

The measurement of lead time follows naturally from set-up reduction and ship-to-WIP. As we noted in Chapter 7, over half of lead time is taken up by queues. We can greatly reduce queue time by shipping directly to the line and even eliminate queues outright in a true JIT environment. Couple queue reduction with set-up reduction and you can readily see that we don't have to accept lead times as unchangeable. Purchasing, by monitoring progress on set-up and queue reduction, plays a large role in shortening lead times. Shorter lead times lead to a higher inventory turnover rate and a greater return on assets. While Purchasing will assist in their own companies, it also is the catalyst which will get suppliers to improve their performance.

Material Handling

How much material handling is required to support production? None __ Minimal __ Moderate __ High __

This measurement can be viewed as a further means to measure the "move" element of lead time. It is also a measurement of the extent to which your company employs group technology, automated storage and retrieval systems, automation or robotics. The same applies to your suppliers' plants as well.

On-Time Delivery

What percentage of supplier deliveries are on time? ___% How is on-time delivery measured to the delivery date?
+/- ___ hours +/- ___ one day +/- ___ five days ___ other (explain)

On-time delivery compares the actual receipt date to the required delivery date. This is obviously an important measurement being that JIT manufacturing relies on just-in-time delivery from suppliers. Remember, however, that early delivery is just as costly as late delivery. If you're receiving parts two or three days ahead of schedule, inventory will rise and you will have to pay the costs of carrying it. The higher the percentage of suppliers delivering on-time and the smaller your delivery window, the closer you come to JIT Purchasing. This is a measurement which needs to be calculated for delivery as a whole and for each individual supplier. Improvement is gained as more and more suppliers come over to JIT delivery.

Customer Delivery Performance

What percentage of your customer deliveries are on-time? ___% How many past due orders are there in terms of dollars ___ and line items ___.

Customer delivery performance is the flip side of on-time delivery. In a JIT environment where a pull system is employed, you manufacture only what you sell. To do otherwise means that you are stockpiling goods in finished goods storerooms. Like on-time delivery, you measure your actual shipping date against the date requested by the customer. Again, this measurement should be broken down by customer and product in order to easily detect where a problem is occurring. Pay attention here to Pareto's law which says that 80% of your customer deliveries will be on-time. The remaining 20% will be the problem area upon which the team's attention should be focused.

We advocate that you establish a goal of a 100% service level. Once established, you measure actual shipping versus the shipping plan on a monthly, quarterly and year-to-date schedule. Remember to include past due orders which should be rolled forward into the current month. Your company's performance should be measured on the sum of past due orders and the current month which will require you to make up the backlog as well as the current month's orders. Inability to do so because of capacity shortages must be addressed by management.

Transportation Costs

What percentage of the price of purchased material is inbound freight? ___% What percentage of sales is outbound freight? ___%

This measurement will make you look more closely at what it costs you to receive material and to ship your product. It will force you to ask yourself the following types of questions:

1. What is the cost of air freight vs. ground transportation?
2. What is the cost of shipping by boat from overseas suppliers?
3. What percentage of your freight is delivered or shipped at priority levels?

The point, obviously, is to reduce your costs and find the most economical method of transportation. As we discussed in Chapter 1, the new role of Purchasing includes functions once placed within the sphere of a separate department, like Traffic or Distribution. But, transportation costs are a significant factor in material procurement and, in the JIT environment, rightfully belong within the sphere of Purchasing. In order to help you compare standard transportation cost to your actual costs, the government has issued a number of publications showing freight rates for various transportation systems.

Inventory Turnover Ratio

How many inventory turns do you get a year? ___ #/yr

The inventory turnover ratio is the forecasted cost of goods sold over the next 12 months divided by the inventory investment.

$$\text{ITR} = \frac{\underline{\text{Forecasted Cost of Goods}}}{\textbf{Inventory Investment}}$$

In our book, *MADE IN AMERICA: The Total Business Concept*, we noted that the measurement of inventory turns is perhaps the single best method for determining the progress of JIT/TQC implementation. Inventory turnovers are something like the Dow Jones Industrial Average in that both act as an overall indicator of the movements of many variables. In the case of the DJIA, these variables are 30 leading industrial companies. In the case of the ITR, these variables are associated with lot sizing, inventory management, line balancing and the Theory of One. We can increase inventory turns by planning for only as much material as a work station needs to make one product and by minimizing queues so that a work station has only enough material to make a product in its cycle time.

Most companies today are struggling to achieve three inventory turns a year. This means they carry four months of inventory. We have worked with companies that have raised the level to 14 turns, 26 turns, 36 turns, even 42 turns a year. Obviously, these companies have been able to coordinate many of the variables mentioned in the paragraph above. Purchasing, once again, can lead the way in the struggle to achieve a higher inventory turnover rate.

Return on Assets

What is your return on asset utilization? ___%

ROA = Net Profits/Total Assets

This is a financial measurement which is viewed differently in the JIT environment. It is not necessary, indeed harmful, to run a machine even if there is no demand. The reasoning is that idle time is expensive and that a major asset such as a machine has to pay for itself by producing parts. The fallacy in this reasoning is that it is based on a "push" system of manufacturing. As we have seen, all this does is stockpile sub-assemblies or finished goods. Warehousing costs money; the cost of carrying inventory costs money. The two costs probably far exceed the cost of idle time. This is not to say that ROA is a useless measurement. It is very useful, given that we plan well and correctly use JIT management techniques. In that situation, where there is little variance between planned and actual, ROA once again becomes valid.

<u>Forecasting Accuracy</u>

What percentage of the time does your forecast reflect actual sales levels? ___%

Planning for production and procurement schedules depends on short-term, accurate forecasting. The closer forecasts are to actual demand, the closer you are to owning one of the basic tenets of JIT, a "pull" system of manufacturing. Another way to measure accuracy is to measure how large or small the error is between the forecast and reality. But be forewarned about this method. Say a company measures a forecast by product group and total dollars and at the end of the year, Marketing announces that they hit the forecast within one percent. They had, within that product group, a major item miss of 30% and another overestimate of 31%. Marketing then says it met its objectives. The two variances almost wash each other out. But what was Production Control doing during this year. They were running around trying to get material to support production or trying to work around material they had no need for.

To remedy this situation, we believe the forecast must be broken down in order to be useful to the whole plant. Marketing needs to get as fine as they can and you should be measuring forecasting error by item, rather than in the aggregate.

Data Accuracy

What is the level of data accuracy (by area; e.g. Bill of Material, Routing, Inventory) ___%

Data accuracy is what we call an "up-front" consideration. There are two reasons for this. One, we exist in a manufacturing environment where change is the only certainty. Take lead time as an example. The one thing we can count on is that if it was 8 days this week, it will be 20 days next week. Thus, it is imperative that our information which we use in planning is up-to-date, as close to a real-time environment as is possible. Two, we can't use up-to-date information that is inaccurate. Amazingly enough, we have heard companies say that every other part that they count in inventory is right on the money. That's only 50 percent; hardly the percentage needed to operate in a JIT environment where pinpoint timing and accurate quantity counts are absolutely necessary. You simply can't forecast, plan, schedule or produce without the most basic of raw materials — accurate information.

Quality Measurements on the Shop Floor

What percentage of your supplier's operations are under the control of Statistical Process Control (SPC)? ___%

In Deming's approach to quality improvement (explained in Chapter 4), he advises companies to "make maximum use of statistical knowledge and talent." Why? Because statistical techniques like SPC are the manufacturing embodiment of the old saying that an ounce of prevention is worth a pound of cure. SPC lets us know when machines are about to produce a bad part before they actually do. This is because statistics allows us to note trends in variances. Once we have noticed assignable variances, we are then able to make changes which insure control over quality.

Another measurement of quality is the percentage of rework. Obviously, if you can predict when a machine will make a bad part or when it needs maintenance, you can reduce rework to negligible levels. Still another quality measurement is the percentage of scrap. This is closely aligned with your Supplier Certification program. The more suppliers enrolled, the less defective material you will receive.

TBC Measurements

If you have noted one dominant theme in our discussion on measurements, it must be the theme of interrelationship. By measuring one area in a JIT environment, you are in effect measuring how well the whole of your company is working. Quality, for example, is also measured by on-time delivery. You don't have an on-time delivery if there are defective parts in the shipment. As another example, let's consider the time it takes to process engineering change orders. Surely, this indicates how well your company is working as a team, but it also indicates how well your relationship with suppliers is working. Remember that earlier, we emphasized that engineering changes are as vital to your suppliers as it is to your production department. After all, suppliers are shipping the material from which you make your product.

This last point brings up another theme of this chapter. Although, we discussed these measurements as ones that you do on your own company, they are the same measurements that you ask your suppliers to use in their companies. They are part of the Supplier Certification Program. They are also the basis for negotiation and even selection of a supplier. Measurements are a rating system that works two ways — they indicate both your performance and your suppliers. We recommend reducing your supplier base and that you reduce based on performance and objectives.

Other TBC performance indicators are the presence of bar coding and preventive maintenance programs. Both indicators show the existence of proactive thought and the automation of repetitive tasks and operations. Like all the other TBC measurements, these indicators also have a theoretical foundation which is remarkably close to the premises underlying the formulation of a new science called Chaos, which is interested in sensitive dependence upon initial conditions. We shall explain because this has much to say about how we measure.

Called the paradox of the butterfly's wings, this premise states that it is impossible to make precise long-range weather forecasts. For a system as complicated as the weather, there is no way for us to take enough measurements to describe current conditions. Hence, we are never sure if the beating of a butterfly's wings in Connecticut will cause a wind storm in southern England.

While we may never know if the whisper of wind around a butterfly grows into a hurricane, we do know that small deviations at Receiving can escalate into major difficulties in Manufacturing and Shipping. By using methods, such as Statistical Process Control or Supplier Certification, which detect these deviations, we can avoid catastrophe.

Donald Trump and Boone Pickens have been categorized as capitalists, but they have the ability to make big companies behave differently. The message that they are trying to get out is that companies must make good products (high quality), involve employees (labor and management) and satisfy the customer.

We would like to leave you with one last thought on how small initial differences can lead to huge resulting differences and why accurate measurement is so essential. As children, we remember reading a short story by Edgar Allan Poe called "The Gold Bug." Briefly, the story is about a treasure hunt in which a gold bug is dropped through the eye socket of a skull lodged high in a tree as the first step in finding the treasure. Once the bug hits the ground, the treasure hunters use that spot to follow the complicated directions which will lead them to the buried jewels and gold coins.

On the first try, the treasure hunters drop the gold bug through the eye socket, make their calculations and dig a hole where they expect the loot to be buried. No luck. Finally, after retracing their

steps, they figure out that they dropped the bug through the wrong eye socket. They climb the tree and proceed to drop the bug through the other socket and eventually find Captain Kidd's buried treasure.

For a child, this story had everything. But, as an adult, it indicates something more. The difference of three inches (the distance between the eye sockets of the skull) became magnified as the treasure hunters moved farther and farther away from the point where the bug hit the ground. A small deviation can make a huge difference. Measuring those small deviations and taking corrective action are what TBC measurements are all about.

CHAPTER NINE: Purchasing and the JIT Team

In a JIT environment, it doesn't matter so much where you start implementation, but that you start. The key to the creation of a framework of continuous improvement is teamwork. Just as farmers in rural sections of our country take a day to raise a barn for a neighbor, teamwork calls for action by all levels of your organization. Thus, the implementation and achievement of JIT consists of four activities:

1. Top Management Commitment
2. Team Administration
3. Training and Education
4. Interdepartmental Cooperation

Only minimal expenditures are needed to improve communication, to involve the workforce in problem-solving and decision-making, or to develop interdepartmental cooperation. And since direct labor works with management on teams, there is an opportunity for both to learn theory (education) and practice techniques (training). With this level of cooperation, learning curves are quickly diminished, thus lowering total cost.

In effect, the creation of a company culture fosters vision, responsibility, authority and accountability. You can think of the above activities as four pillars which support a roof. Take away one pillar and the structure crashes to the ground. We are now ready to delve into the most important part of the construction. We have the architectural plans for JIT Purchasing.

Purchasing's Role

Purchasing is uniquely positioned within a company to play a leading role in JIT implementation since, in many companies, materials procurement exceeds 60-70% of product cost. It's role is not limited either to the procurement of material or to the adoption of JIT as a manufacturing philosophy by the company.

Purchasing must be an advocate of the Total Business Concept. It must achieve the desired result of 100% good quality, 100% of the time. In addition, it must bring together as one the tasks of company integration and supplier involvement.

Purchasing must be like a professional artist drawing a picture. Good artists, like Dick Maccabe, are able to draw well because they are trained to see not only the object they are drawing but also the boundary of the space which surrounds the object. The line they draw on a sheet of paper is as much a rendering of the space around a vase of flowers as it is a rendering of the flowers themselves. They are able to tie the object and its surroundings together so that the vase does not float about or appear distorted without reason. Purchasing should be able to do the same. It should be able to draw the line which makes a picture connecting internal and external company activities, to create, in other words, a supplier partnership.

We believe that you should tend to your own backyard before you go out and convince others that they must change. We are reminded of a story about how Missouri came to be known as the "Show Me! State." Seems like a politician from the state went to a national convention and listened to the leaders brag about what they had done for the country and what they would do. This politician listened and listened and when it came his turn to speak, he got up to the rostrum, looked at the crowd, and hollered, "Show Me!"

Don't let this situation ever develop with your suppliers. Don't tell them how great and wonderful JIT is unless you are able to produce results in your own plant. And the way to get these results is to develop teamwork through JIT teams and with top management commitment as will be discussed in the next chapter.

What is a JIT Team?

A team is a group dedicated to a common goal, who rely on each other's strengths and fill in for each other's weaknesses.

The results of a team will be greater than the sum of efforts made by individuals. As we pointed out in our book, *Made In America*, much of JIT has a gestalt, or holistic, effect. Even though your company is made up of semi-autonomous parts, they add up to a whole. This is especially true in a JIT environment where we have what we call a spider-web effect; an action in one area affects all areas. When you put the gestalt and spider-web effects together, you have a team which can see internal and external aspects of your company and the reverberations caused by actions in one department as they ripple through the company as a whole.

Few people, perhaps only geniuses, are capable of perceiving these two effects simultaneously. Teams, however, are made up of individuals from a number of disciplines within your company and even from your suppliers. Thus, when a team sets out to solve a problem, there are inputs from a number of areas, each of which states how possible solutions will effect them. Hypotheses and plans of action are made by a group process which has been documented as producing more participation. Undoubtedly, participation and the efficacy of suggestions increases because of our need, described in *In Search of Excellence*, to be a part of a team as well as an individual.

Team Structure and Member Selection

The first step in team-building is to form a steering committee. The steering committee should be an interdepartmental team consisting of 6-8 people from the areas of Engineering, Design, Sales, Marketing, Production, Purchasing and Finance as well as labor. It would also be wise at this time to include a union representative to impress upon members the importance and necessity of flexibility.

The steering committee involves itself in the preparatory phase of the JIT journey:

1. Exposure to JIT through orientation and education.
2. Preparation of an opportunity and readiness assessment in terms of talent internal and external to your company.
3. Development of a future company vision and first year action plan through planning sessions.

The steering committee then forms JIT teams, the first step in the implementation phase of the JIT journey. (see chart on p.) Project teams, as the name implies, coalesce around certain projects brought to attention by the steering committee. In a typical implementation, we recommend four to five teams of 8-10 people.

The actual rules or plans of action are the job of a JIT team working within the guidelines of the steering committee. The steering committee is a catalyst. It defines what JIT means to the company, reviews projects, provides resources and guides the overall problem-solving effort. Another way to put this is to say that the steering committee creates the culture for change and maintains that environment.

If the steering committee is the strategy maker, then the JIT team finds ways to implement that strategy. Any JIT team, then, really has only one overall mandate — investigate symptoms, identify the causes (problems), identify the means to solve the problem and implement the solution which eliminates the problem.

The composition of a JIT team should be 50% direct labor and 50% management from both the supplier and your company. Certainly, you need people on the team with expertise. You also need people with little knowledge but with the ability to never be satisfied. There is something to say for "naive" members, the ones who ask all the "dumb" questions. For example: "Why do you do it this way?" We call this team process, DSE, or Different Set of Eyes. Recently, we came across an article in *The Atlantic* **(1)** which confirms our belief in the inclusion of a member with fresh insight.

Paul Erdös is a mathematician without a home. He carries his two or three shirts, socks, underwear and pants around the world in a battered valise. He is always on the lookout for teaming up with other mathematicians to solve problems. He will appear at a fellow mathematician's door and announce that he is staying to work. When he is finished, he leaves and travels to another doorstep whether that is across town or across oceans. He is without doubt an eccentric character who survives because of his fellow professionals' care and respect for his genius. Despite his unorthodox ways, he has authored or co-authored over 1,000 papers, all of them important mathematical works.

What does he have to do with team member selection? Paul Erdös is one of those people who always asks and answers the "dumb" questions, the questions that are so obvious that no one sees them. Paul Erdös, even at 70 years of age (ancient by mathematical standards where it is usually believed that if you don't publish something important by 30, you never will), has an amazing ability to maintain an insight which is consistently fresh. That's the type of person you want on a team.

Selecting team members with fresh insight is one way to break down existing barriers in your company. Another way is to expose JIT teams to the full range of problems. The idea behind teamwork is to expand the base of experience, so that no one team, for example, becomes known as the team responsible for quality.

Quality is everybody's responsibility. Thus, you should make sure that quality problems are rotated from JIT team to JIT team. The same holds true for any other class of problems such as communication, morale, safety, preventive maintenance, set-up reduction, etc.

Another way to break down barriers and maintain freshness is to adopt an open-door policy. At one of our client's, L'Oréal Cosmetics (Cosmair), for example, there were gray doors separating the office from the factory floor. One of the first activities of the JIT team at the plant was to create an environment where the doors were no longer a barrier. Their rationale was that open doors create an environment for open minds.

At the same Cosmair plant, Gerry Price, vice president of manufacturing, volunteered to work two days a month on the production line. And he did, from 7:30 a.m. to 3:30 p.m., with no phone calls allowed and only scheduled breaks and lunch time. He was heard to remark after the first day that "this is hard work." He admitted to a profound change in his views. Needless to say, line workers were far more apt to listen to a vice president who had worked in the trenches. Again, this is the type of management player you want on your team. Somebody willing to get their hands dirty.

Besides the abilities to question and to be open and the qualities of energy, excitement and experience, team members must be given the proper decision-making authority and responsibility to make changes, if they do not already have this power. Since your teams will ideally have an equal number of direct laborers and management, you will have to show workers that you mean what you say. Giving direct labor equal representation, of course, says more than mere words. We have found this technique to be particularly effective in encouraging participation and overcoming workers' fears in the face of management. In short, the same non-adversarial quality which determines supplier relationships should also determine the relationship between management and direct labor.

At Cosmair, for instance, one worker who initially spoke out against certain facets of JIT was intentionally picked to be on a JIT team. At first, he could not understand why and did not participate while attending meetings. But, in one meeting, the team began talking about reducing set-up time. This worker then got up and came up with an idea for eliminating wasteful steps in his area. At the end of the meeting, he told us he now understood why he was on the team. He is now an enthusiastic supporter of change.

Team Rules and Objectives

There are inherent problems with teams. Whenever a lot of cooks are stirring the broth, there will be arguments over what ingredients are best. How do you form and manage a JIT team in which you reap the benefits of a diverse group while not stifling individual creativity? How can Purchasing sit down with Marketing, Engineering, Production and Quality and come up with integrated solutions? How do you create a team?

The answer comes in four parts. One, you need to establish ground rules, goals, objectives and a sense of direction. Two, you need to educate and train all levels of your company and your supplier in JIT. Three, you must teach JIT teams how to administer the formation and implementation of the action plans. Four, you must initiate program reviews and provide ongoing support. All of these four parts are the work of the steering committee and JIT teams tackling problems together. They are also done inside your plant through the cooperation of several departments and outside your plant through the creation of a partnership with your suppliers.

Let's look first at the establishment of rules and objectives. The overall goals of JIT teams are the same as those we have repeatedly emphasized for all facets of JIT. Purchasing must infuse a sense of vision, responsibility, authority and accountability in the group which gathers to work on a task. We must move toward a manufacturing environment in which the previously separate areas of buying and planning merge into the role of the buyer/planner. In many companies, this could transform the role of shipping and receiving as that department begins to work directly with the production department and suppliers. In other words, JIT

Purchasing is a process of fusion, rather than fission. Energy is created as different departments work closer and closer together, as the barriers between them slowly break down, just as our sun creates energy by fusing hydrogen atoms into ones of helium. In the process of fusion, your company will move from ignorance and confusion about JIT Purchasing to the adoption of a JIT mind-set.

A Supplier Partnership

The same process of fusion should also happen with suppliers. We have discovered in our work with clients around the world that there are seven objectives in the process of creating a partnership with suppliers:

- Reduce set-up times.
- Improve frequency of deliveries.
- Eliminate waste in supplier's plant.
- Seek simplicity in solutions.
- Work for continuous improvement.
- Communicate results and make them visible.
- Develop inventory turn objectives.

This is the foundation upon which you will create a sense of teamwork. At a recent seminar, we came across a perfect example of a company, a supplier, who is trying to become qualified in another company's Supplier Certification Program. Paris Art Label supplies one of our clients, Cosmair, with specialty packaging for their products. We were pleasantly surprised to see the vice president of Art Label at our seminar on Supplier Certification. Most of the other participants were representatives of companies who wanted to implement a certification program. Art Label's vice president represented a supplier which wanted to know what supplier certification was and, most importantly, how to work with a company requesting its suppliers to become certified.

The vice president agreed with the above objectives. He saw the value of working as a team with the company he was supplying. We cite this example because many companies believe that suppliers will automatically balk when asked to set the objectives above. They won't as long as both the supplier and the manufacturer work together.

At the same time these objectives are assimilated and become second nature through education and open discussion at your supplier, you should be setting objectives like the ones below at your own company for internal JIT teams.

THE TEN-STEP PLAN

1. Avoid studying or planning a project to death
2. Don't be satisfied with early successes
3. Don't get tangled up in techniques
4. Always strive for continuous goal improvements
5. Make problems, goals, accomplishments visible to all
6. Document all steps of your progress
7. Believe in "small is beautiful"
8. Eliminate waste in your plant
9. Seek simplicity in solutions
10. Develop inventory turn objectives

Now that you have common objectives both internally and externally, you are ready to begin education and training.

Education and Training

Education is learning the theory behind what you are doing; training is putting into practice what you have learned. Education must occur at all levels of a company as well as in the supplier's plant. Contrary to traditional educational methods used by many companies where more time is spent teaching direct labor than management, we invert the educational pyramid as shown on the next page.

This plan is for the stage where you educate your company and your suppliers about JIT Purchasing. Top management receives more extensive education because without their understanding

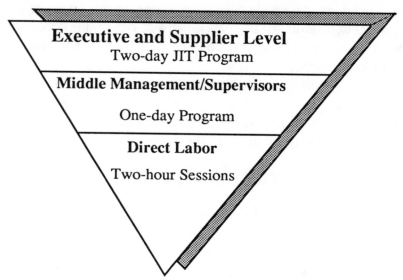

Executive and Supplier Level
Two-day JIT Program

Middle Management/Supervisors

One-day Program

Direct Labor

Two-hour Sessions

and commitment, the rest of your education and training program will go nowhere. It is an undeniable fact that workers look to their leaders for direction. A middle manager is far more apt to embrace JIT if she sees a vice president genuinely committed to it.

Training is a tool to help your business meet its objectives today and in the future. The responsibility for ensuring that a company's staff and a supplier are properly trained and competent rests with the Purchasing Manager. Your goal, then, is to provide a positive atmosphere which will stimulate employees to discuss theory, practices and alternatives. You should base training on job competency and focus it on creating greater cross-functional awareness. Training and education must become a way of life in your company. Some companies, for example, always have some structured activities for their workers whenever a line shuts down. We recommend that you use down-time to instruct employees in more problem-solving techniques, in reviewing Statistical Process results or in improving process change-overs. It's a way of life whose end result is to give workers the tools for continuous improvement.

The first priority in planning a training and education program in JIT Purchasing in your plant and for suppliers is to assess needs and opportunities. We have developed a competency model which will assist you in defining where your company is proficient and deficient. You should use this model as a guide. The numbers indicate the necessary levels of expertise for each function. By comparing the levels of expertise within your company to the desired levels in the chart, you can determine short-term and long-term objectives in your education and training program.

Competency Model for Determining Knowledge and Skill Requirements By Function

COMPETENCY AREAS	FUNCTIONS							
	Marketing	Finance	Sales	Production	Quality	Purchasing	Planning	Traffic
JIT Principles	3	3	3	3	3	3	3	3
Set-up Reduction	1	2	1	3	3	3	3	1
Supplier Certification	2	1	2	3	3	3	3	3
SPC/TQC	1	1	1	3	3	3	3	2
Preventive Maint.	1	1	1	3	1	1	2	1
Value Analysis	1	1	1	3	3	3	3	2
Problem-solving	3	3	3	3	3	3	3	3
MRP II	2	3	2	3	2	3	3	3

1. indicates a familiarity with subject
2. requires a working knowledge of field
3. requires expertise in area

Once you have these objectives accurately developed, you can begin to develop a schedule of training and education which suits your particular needs. A sample training and education program is given on the next page.

As for the course content itself, it should include the following approach for successful company/supplier involvement:

1. Principles and techniques.
2. How to study.

3. Objectives.
4. Focus on theory.
5. Case studies.
6. Historical and current perspectives.
7. Company differences.
8. Interface requirements.

EDUCATION AND TRAINING
ACTIVITY PLAN

Activity	Time Periods									
	1	2	3	4	5	6	7	8	9	10
Assess needs	x									
Evaluate competence	x	x								
Develop preliminary plan		x								
Prepare budget		x								
Obtain management support		x								
Develop steering committee	x									
Develop project team		x	x							
Outline course plan			x							
Develop program measurements			x							
Train the trainers			x							
Hold pilot model courses				x						
Schedule education courses *					x					
Schedule training courses					x					
Measure results					x	x	x	x	x	x
Measure JIT performance results							x	x	x	x
Revise program as required								x	x	x

* SPC, Set-up Reduction, Supplier Cerrtification

Management of the JIT/Supplier Team

The stage is set for implementing and managing the tasks which will lead to JIT Purchasing and the creation of a partnership with suppliers. The JIT team Process begins with a needs and readiness assessment to evaluate the current status of the task team's area of inquiry and the opportunities which are present. This assessment should include the following actions:

1. Create a business vision statement (objectives)
2. Identify opportunities for improvement

    3. Structure organization for success

    4. Identify existing and required skills inventory

    5. Assess climate/political environment

    6. Determine impact of existing company culture

    7. Develop plan to implement process

This will undoubtedly result in a long list of areas in which to work on improvement. The second step is to prioritize the list. The third step is to make a timetable which defines the tasks identified in the implementation plan. Each task must show its dependency on the completion of another task and schedule. Be sure to establish beginning and end dates. We have found that without a start date, tasks may not be completed on time.

Once the tasks and people are identified and the timetables established, your next task is to establish regular team meetings. It is imperative that meetings should not be cancelled and that there should be 100% attendance. Nothing stops the momentum of team interaction more quickly than one or two cancelled meetings. Members immediately start to question your commitment to solving problems. Indeed, a measure of a company's commitment will be whether it will support two hours of involvement per week for each person.

Using the guidelines of the Task Team Process, you are now ready to go through a five-step process which will aid you in the development of an action plan.

ACTION PLAN PROCESS

        Plan Development
        Execution
        Measurement
        Evaluation
        Corrective Action

This process is similar to the scientific method we were taught early in our careers. You have gathered facts about symptoms and their true, underlying causes. Like a scientist, you devise a hypothesis which attempts to explain why there is a problem and how to eliminate it. This hypothesis is the product of the PLAN-NING phase. You then EXECUTE that plan, or test your hypothesis. Based on the execution, you gather data on the test and MEASURE what is happening. Then, you EVALUATE your measurements against the plan's original goal. Did your hypothesis predict the phenomena correctly? Invariably, there will be some variance between the predicted and the actual results, leading you to take CORRECTIVE ACTION and start the cycle over again. Eventually, you come to a point where your latest hypothesis correctly identifies the source of the problem and installs a superior alternative.

One last rule about JIT teams and their administration. The best managed teams are those in which improvement does not end with the completion of the project and in which the improvement guidelines have been developed by the team itself. This internally developed approach, which can be aided by the services of outside consultants, creates a greater sense of ownership, acceptance and commitment within the team and throughout the company. It is true that there are basic rules for managing companies which appear everywhere. Nevertheless, there are differences in culture, attitude and company history which makes an internally developed program far more effective since the form of the process matches the content of the company.

Group Facilitation Training

Now that you have assembled a JIT team, it would be unwise to set them loose on your company's problems automatically. There are still two steps to take before this is possible. First you must train the group in the dynamics of group processes and second, you must train them in problem-solving techniques.

Teams most often fail because they have not been trained in how to work together as a group. Such questions as how to increase participation or select a leader are left to the group to decide. An important impetus to participate comes in the team selection step where a varied team in terms of departments and levels in the company hierarchy almost assures lively discussions. At this point, it may be time to include your suppliers on the team.

Equally important is to create an environment in which everybody can speak without fear of reprisal. A client learned this point very well. A JIT team consisting of workers on a production line and a vice president stopped their work one day and called a meeting. The meeting was about two line workers who were not pulling their weight. Rather than embarrass these workers in front of management, the team chose to handle the problem by itself. How many companies in America have this atmosphere of trust? Trust is vital to team participation and success.

Our number one lesson comes as another acronym — LSL, or Leader Speaks Last. A manager should allow less skilled or lower level people to talk during meetings. The senior person should only speak when called upon, when the group comes to an impasse or at the end of the meeting. When that person does talk, it should only be to lend expertise or to ease the process. In short, leaders should never dominate a meeting. This only limits the number of possible solutions as team members either wait for or are afraid of the leader and his position. Leaders tend to state their views which are blindly followed. We want to avoid this mistake.

Problem-Solving

The JIT team is in place and ready to function, but they need one more lesson — training in problem-solving. The first rule is to narrow a team's focus to those problems which only add value to a product or eliminate waste. Refusing to narrow a team's focus was often the failure of quality circles as well as not being given the authority and responsibility to solve a whole range of problems without special management approval. We have often encountered teams who have helped their companies immeasurably simply by moving testing equipment closer to a production line. Of course, there is a danger in becoming overly concerned with the workplace environment. For that reason, we recommend that team members receive at least one hour of training in problem identification and then apply problem-solving techniques every week during team meetings. Without this time commitment, we wonder if there is true management commitment.

There are several problem-solving techniques, but they all employ a method which seeks to avoid common pitfalls. These pitfalls are:

1. Jumping to conclusions.
2. Imposing our own pet solutions.
3. Only "wounding" the problem instead of "killing" it.
4. Thinking we know the answers to all the questions.

To avoid doing the above, we stress:

1. Separating cause from effect.
2. Thinking through the problem objectively and logically.
3. Stepping back and looking for "root" causes, not just what may appear to be obvious.

One effective problem-identification technique is the cause and effect (fishbone) diagram as shown below. The intent is to identify a problem and its possible causes and then to note which causes are being worked on and which are done.

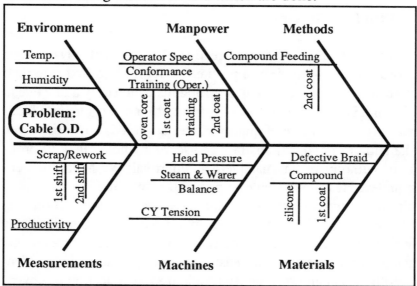

Cause Enumeration Fishbone

In our example, you can undoubtedly see that one problem may have causes in a number of areas. For example, is "inaccurate measurement" a machine problem, a measurement problem or a manpower problem? It is not so important where you place the problem on the fishbone as it is to identify the problem and causes. If you spend too much time deciding what goes where, you could contract the dreaded disease of "paralysis through analysis". Earlier in this chapter, we warned you not to study a plan to death. Problem-solving is more than identification; it is action.

The actual problem-solving is governed by three steps. In step one, we divide a sheet into three columns with the following headings:

Observable Symptom
Possible Causes
Verify the Causes

Real problems are seldom observable. That is why we take care to separate symptoms from causes. It is in the listing of possible causes that the team process comes into its own. If a team is given the freedom to brainstorm, to be thorough and objective, it will avoid applying time-worn band-aids. We are looking for the causes of a symptom to which we will apply the solutions. A successful technique is to ask the question "why?" five times (5W's). Once we have verified the causes, we now have the problems identified. Correctly identifying the problem, in many instances, is half the battle.

In step two, we ask team members to write the problem statement at the top of another sheet. We suggest that they start the statement with the phrase: "Must find a way to eliminate ..." Once they have stated the problem, then the team members brainstorm again and identify at least five possible solutions. Remember that these solutions must be able to "kill" the problem.

In step three, we test the hypotheses just formulated and map out the steps needed to implement each solution as well as estimates of costs and human resource requirements. By this time, the optimal solution should become quite clear. It is the lowest cost one.

Rewards, Recognition and Incentives

The end product of JIT teams is to generate ideas or recommendations with accompanying action plans. But it is a basic characteristic of humans that they will not continue an activity if it is not recognized. And recognition must be more than unlocking a "suggestion box" and awarding one prize to the best idea while throwing the other ideas into the round file. The best run companies in America are willing to follow through on ideas which may end in failure. These companies are not afraid to include the word "failure" in their vocabulary. They know, like Isaac Newton knew, that we only stand on the shoulders of those who came before us. That means not only on their accomplishments, but on their failures because failures tell us as much as accomplishments. Failures tell us where not to go or they spin off other questions and problems which may lead to far greater successes.

Thus, your company needs to create an environment where it is safe to make suggestions. No suggestion, no question, is unimportant. Toyota Motor Corp., for example, has developed a "creative suggestion system" in which its "non-management 55,000-strong work force contributed over 2.649 million improvement proposals" in 1986. (2) The Mazda Co. in 1987 received 350,000 suggestions from its 800 employees. Obviously, it is safe to suggest changes in these companies. Besides having an open-minded attitude, these companies also act quickly on the given suggestions. Every idea is distributed to the appropriate team or department for action. In addition, we recommend taking "bad" suggestions (which may be suggestions which are not clearly described) and using them in training sessions where you teach company employees how to make more effective suggestions.

The premise behind suggestions is to make the company receptive to change because it is only through change that you will improve. This attitude demonstrates to your workers that the company is supporting the JIT/TQC program. They begin to see that your company views its workers as important and knowledgeable people. This recognition is only strengthened by a reward system which recognizes the value of the team. Toyota, for example, does not greatly vary the amount of a cash reward based on its economical benefit to the company. They reason that rewards for even the most sketchy of ideas "create greater incentive for further contribution of ideas and encourage more extensive participation in the program." The results are impressive. Japanese workers average 24 suggestions per year to only 0.14 suggestions for American workers. **(3)**

Pete and Mike remember very well the extra couple of hours a day spent with other young managers brainstorming suggestions at the Stanley Works in New Britain in the early sixties. Their group came up with enough ideas for many members to purchase items normally beyond their budgets. In 1971, when Jerry Claunch worked for Lennox Heating and Air Conditioning in Des Moines, Iowa, they had a program where 10% of all savings generated by 65 volunteers in value analysis was equally distributed among the participants.

Needless to say, both were very worthwhile programs and the rewards were clearly tied to the suggestion-making effort. Some such type of reward, bonus or profit-sharing plan is still the most effective way to recognize achievement above and beyond the call of duty. For every dollar saved, we strongly recommend that at least 10 to 15 cents be given directly back to the program. For larger projects which involve the whole company, this percentage of the savings should be across the board. At Apple's Macintosh plant, for instance, the whole work force was given 25% of their salary as a bonus if we were able to manufacture "x" number of computers by a certain date. Talk about teamwork! This was something everybody could work toward and share in.

Common Questions and Problems

We now come to questions and problems which arise from the implementation of JIT teams. The following questions are actual queries which came up at a meeting of a Communication Team at a client's plant.

1. What do you do when everything that goes wrong is blamed on JIT?

Ask yourself if you did a thorough job in educating all levels of the company in JIT. Did you explain that there may be an initial upswing in whatever item you are measuring or observing as problems are revealed for the first time?

2. Should you select employees or should they volunteer as team members?

A good question which is difficult to answer. We aren't avoiding the question by saying that it depends on the circumstances. We found, for instance, that selecting the non-believers at some clients was beneficial. There is also much to say for letting employees volunteer or by letting teams coalesce around a champion. Whatever the case, you should make sure that the team has a varied make-up, different sets of eyes and a policy where the leader is not a person who may tend to dominate proceedings and stifle participation. This may require training in the group facilitation process.

3. How do you treat all employees equally when they have different levels of knowledge, reading ability, math and writing skills?

Consider remedial education as part of the training and education process. If you think remedial education is expensive, try ignorance. Also, don't patronize less skilled workers by "passing" someone who doesn't make the grade. Don't fire them either — the word will spread. Don't pretend that everyone is equal; the employees know it isn't true and they will not trust you in other areas if you pretend otherwise. Face the issue of different abilities squarely in the face. You will gain much respect if you do.

4. How do you deal with people who haven't been picked for a team and wanted to be?

We should all be so lucky. It's a situation similar to the one faced by a coach who has to keep a team from peaking too early. Explain the situation as Bill Russell of the Boston Celtics used to: you're one spoke in the wheel; perhaps today you won't play, but you're still needed to keep the wheel from collapsing. If we win the championship and all you did was keep the starters sharp by playing hard in practice, then you were just as important to our victory as the star was.

5. What about the situation where people won't sign up?

If you have done a good initial job in educating your company in JIT and you have shared vital information with them and stressed survival and jobs, then you should have little trouble with getting people on your side. If you still have trouble, then be honest and have a meeting in which you discuss why there is so much reluctance. This may be a trust issue and the only way you can deal with it is through open and honest confrontation.

6. How can we make our communication more effective?

The simple answer is to do everything we suggested in this chapter and to be honest and open. Other suggestions are to publish an in-house newsletter. The key here is visibility. Performance charts indicating progress could be placed on walls. In other words, a little publicity. Communication does not come quickly and, like advertising, the best way to get results is through word-of-mouth. If you are moving in the right direction and make sure everybody knows you are, people will come to you and to each other.

7. How do you get everyone at a team meeting to talk and participate?

Make sure that you have trained your employees in the group facilitation process and that the team is not led by someone who dominates or stifles creativity. Other suggestions are to make sure that the team is talking about a subject they are interested in and that they chose instead of having it forced upon them. Also, improve the team's problem-solving skills. Perhaps the problem is too large. Break a problem down into more manageable parts. Brainstorm. Take a break. Create sub-cells to address part of the problem.

If you still have a problem with participation, then address it directly. Sometimes, lack of participation is a passive/aggressive behavior. In other words, workers get back at the company by not doing anything to help. Find out what is behind this behavior. Perhaps a lack of trust in the company? resentment over past policies? Air out those problems first. If you do, you start to show your trustworthiness and subsequently build a support network.

8. What should we do if a problem starts to come to a head and then we either run out of time or there is a lack of priority?

Define your goals and timetables precisely and realistically. Don't expend 80% of your effort and time on the first 20% of your task. If this is a problem because of a lack of top management commitment, address the problem directly with the team and management. You may need more education in JIT Purchasing to convince people that this work is important.

9. What kind of reward system should we use and how?

We recommend that you ask your employees what they want as a realistic reward. Management often finds this topic difficult because it is hard to know what satisfies everybody. All the more reason, then, to involve the team in the process of selecting a reward system. With employees, rewards may come as money, recognition or both. With suppliers, it might be payment terms or cash for on-time delivery. Remember: If you give a little, you may get a lot.

10. How do we get people interested in the company?

Employees' interest in your company begins with top management commitment to a culture that accepts change. That is where teamwork gets the energy to sustain itself. And with teamwork comes interest.

CHAPTER TEN: Management Commitment for JIT Purchasing

We have heard about top management commitment since the early days of MRP II project implementations. But, in all that time in which we have listened, we never let ourselves think that, maybe, top management is the people who work in a company. People need to establish a sense of ownership before they are ready to be held accountable for the success or failure of a task. We must provide an environment where people have the opportunity to fail as well as succeed. Suppliers, too, must be involved. No longer can we accept an approach which deals with them as adversaries.

Another necessary element for top management commitment is the need to change attitudes. The people who work in our companies must start to view the company not as a place to work but as an environment in which they can contribute to the company's success and profit picture. Jack Welch of General Electric has this to say:

> "Once the boss is in place, it is his job to 'develop a vision' for the business ... and oversee a change in culture to accomplish it." **(1)**

How do we get people interested in the company? It is a question which forms the keystone between two sides of an arch. On one side of the arch, we have the formation and administration of project and supplier teams to effect JIT Purchasing. On the other side is top management commitment and the creation of a company culture which fosters responsibility, authority, vision and accountability. This encompasses all people. There must exist a commonalty of purpose, goals and direction, a keystone, to maintain the arch's strength.

Purchasing's role is to facilitate the simultaneous building of both sides of that arch. All the effort put into project and supplier teams will be for naught if there isn't an environment which accepts change. Most important is the change required by Finance in its measurement of successful purchasing. Traditional accounting methods, for example, measure according to Purchase Price Variance (PPV). Management, in numerous American companies, requires Purchasing to obtain three quotes. This process is price-driven, not total cost-driven as JIT requires. Purchasing people get rewarded on price which is compared to a standard.

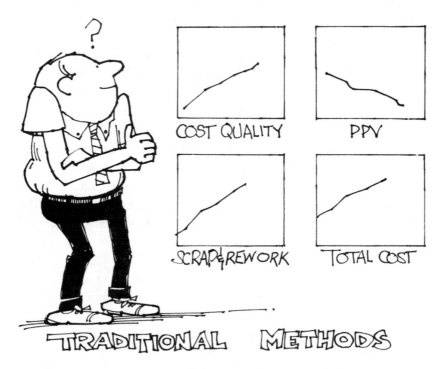

Certainly the most compelling reasons for management to consider JIT Purchasing is to lower total cost and to face the threat of competition, both domestic and foreign. America could use more top management people who subscribe to what General Motors Corp. Chairman Roger Smith said recently in *USA Today*:

> We're not afraid of competition. I'd rather see the jobs here than in Japan. The union and all the auto companies are working as hard as they can together to beat the competition. One of the great things the Japanese did for us was to make management and labor work together like they never did before.

We need only add the supplier network, internal employee involvement and customers to Smith's statement and there is a start for the culture and commitment we are looking for. Commitment reminds us of a ham and egg sandwich. The chicken participated, but the pig was committed.

Purchasing, we believe, is in a unique position to provide management with the information to fill out the skeleton of commitment. Because of its involvement in procuring material for production, Purchasing has first-hand knowledge of the ways in which JIT can mean the difference between success and failure. Purchasing managers are also, in effect, mini-plant managers for dozens, even hundreds of manufacturing sites. With so much information, Purchasing is able to drive the total cost of the product in the proper direction. We need to give form to commitment and to crack open the closet door. The creature that comes out does not necessarily have to be a Frankenstein. The chairman of General Motors didn't see it that way.

It would serve us well to remember that the original Frankenstein in Mary Shelly's book was not inherently evil. He was neither good, nor bad. But, because he was abandoned by his creator and feared by people, Frankenstein became a monster. There is no reason why we should let JIT and the threat of foreign competition become Frankensteins, if we do not abandon our commitment, if we do not fear striving for partnership at all levels.

What is Top Management Commitment?

Let's define top management commitment and the accompanying culture change which occurs as you implement the JIT process. Indeed, perhaps one of the most important ingredients of management commitment is the acceptance that there will be change and that change is essential to progress. Progress starts with this question:

WHAT ARE WE DOING AND WHY ARE WE DOING IT?

Management must ask the above question and accept answers which may be difficult to hear. Only then is a company on its way to improvement. Top management commitment means creating an environment where creative problem-solving is the norm. And JIT, we believe, exposes the true causes of problems better than any other business philosophy. Furthermore, JIT demands that you squarely confront the most difficult task of management — listening to people.

If listening is top management's most difficult task, then management must subscribe to the following requirements and actions:

TOP MANAGEMENT COMMITMENT REQUIREMENTS

- Establishing goals and objectives
- Patience and persistence in working with people
- Develop a trust with your people, suppliers and customers
- Delegation of responsibility, authority, vision and accountability to the operator level

DEMONSTRATED ACTIONS OF A COMMITTED TOP MANAGEMENT

- Adopt a no-waste attitude
- Allocate/authorize financial support and measurements
- Devote resources to project teams
- Risk short-term operational results for long-term improvements
- Foster interdepartmental communication and cooperation
- Follow up, monitor, document and measure
- Establish an on-going training and education program
- Improve communications with suppliers and customers
- Listen to the experts — your people
- Correct processes, rather than rework parts
- Foster a "no waiver" environment in processes and specifications

The people who work in our companies want to see a committed top management. The following example shows a company where there is no commitment to the above and shows how a company could change its procedures to demonstrate commitment.

A component from a supplier arrives at Company X's (with no JIT) receiving room prior to inspection. The component is subsequently rejected by the inspector for a particular problem. The component is then sent to the MRB (Material Review Board) cage where it sits and waits for a decision to be made. In many companies, the component just sits there and, by some process that we don't quite understand, gets better. Actually, we do know what happens. Components are sorted and selected and the bad ones returned to the supplier.

In Company Y (with JIT), the philosophy is not to store items in MRB area, but to get suppliers involved in a certification program which will insure the delivery of zero-defect components. Along the way to that goal, management must show its commitment. Now, when a component arrives and gets rejected by Inspection, management starts to ask questions. The first question is "Can we use it?" If the answer is "yes," then change the specifications. Sometimes, your specifications are much more stringent than they need to be. For example, we have come across companies that will reject parts because the paint job has imperfections, even though this part is assembled into a product and never sees the light of day again. If the specifications can't be changed, then reject the component and stop the line.

This is management commitment. How many American companies follow this procedure? Our competition abroad does. It follows the rule of 100% good parts, 100% of the time or it fixes the problem.

How to Obtain Management Commitment

A successful way to gain top management commitment is with information about the bottom-line savings. Total cost, not actual supplier cost, is the important criterion here. There are three ways in which you can make management listen. One way is to forward every article, book, report and piece of information about the tangible benefits of JIT to the top levels of your company. A second way is to arrange for on-site visits to plants which have embraced JIT so management can see a total business concept in action. Jerry Claunch remembers that there were so many requests for visits to the Kawasaki plant when he worked there that a limit had to be imposed. This provided a learning experience for all. The third way is to select a small part of your company and implement a pilot project before tackling the whole. The pilot project must yield quick results or else we will risk losing management commitment.

In the case of the last suggestion, we recommend choosing an area with the most visible paybacks. It could be an area which is most in need of improvement and/or it could be one in which you are assured of success. Whatever the area, your eye for success should not exceed the capacity of your stomach to digest what you have undertaken. In other words: Don't bite off more than you can chew. Your goal here is not to turn the company around, but to demonstrate the bottom-line savings possible. The time must be short, but the results dramatic.

Top management must also develop an implementation plan executed by the project teams. In addition, a steering committee should be established, consisting of people from Engineering, Marketing, Production, Purchasing and Finance. Its responsibility is to direct the overall effort of JIT implementation. Top management must provide resources, power and authority to the project teams.

Education, of course, is critical to the attainment of JIT. Our approach to education differs from the norms of executive briefings. For years, executives have been briefed on a plethora of subjects with very few results. We propose that top management spend more time in the education process than the rest of the plant as we depicted in the educational pyramid.

The inverted pyramid emphasizes that top management must be committed to education. It is an undeniable fact that a company looks to its leaders for direction. Middle management is always ready to embrace a program if upper management is committed. People at lower levels in the company are ready to accept change, provided they are given the responsibility and authority to act and that there is direction from above. But, we need to overcome accepted practices which have conditioned top management to make all the decisions. JIT requires Purchasing, suppliers and, in some cases, the suppliers' suppliers to work as a TEAM. In some industries, Marketing and customers should also be involved.

Top management commitment is really no more than a commitment to continuous improvement. To get there means taking what we call the Total Business Approach, a journey from exposure through orientation and education to program review and on-going support. The chart on the next page shows an approach in which Purchasing works with the supplier network.

The left side of the chart shows the Development/Preparation phase. It consists of three steps: Education, Supplier Readiness and Development of an Action Plan. Management's involvement in this phase is to provide guidance, vision and direction to the implementation teams.

The right side of the chart is the Implementation Process phase which consists of six steps. Management commitment here is exemplified by the provision of the budget, time and resources to make the project successful. Tom Peters and Robert Waterman, in *In Search of Excellence*, state that successful management follows the MBWA approach — Management by Walking Around. We would like to add that LSL — Leader Speaks Last — and DSE — Different Set of Eyes — are equally important in this phase. We require all disciplines to be involved, not just people who work in a particular area. We want people to ask the question "WHY?" at least five times. What shouldn't happen is management dictating what they want to see as the answer.

Budgets, Money and Support

JIT Purchasing requires a budget to support travel to suppliers, tooling, capital equipment and supplier quality engineering. In

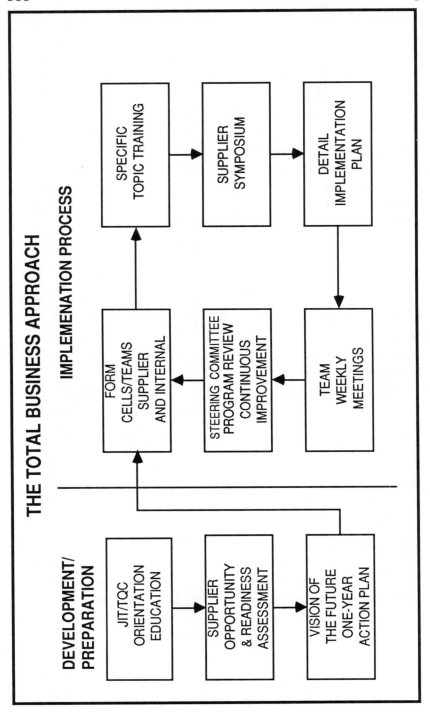

some instances, the budget also involves education and training programs such as Statistical Process Control or Just-In-Time concepts.

As for travel to suppliers, we have found that a partnership will not develop unless an adequate amount of time is spent with a supplier. At many of our seminars, we have seen that more than 80% of the purchasing people visit their supplier less than two times a year. Good suppliers receive even less visits. How can a partnership develop under these conditions?

Tooling requires constant monitoring of produced parts to insure quality control over fixtures, new tooling, set-up reduction and lot size reduction. Purchasing's role is to provide the suppliers with support in these areas so that inventory reduction is possible. Always keep this order in mind, however, when attacking the problem. First, set-up reduction, then lot size reduction, then inventory reduction. Budgets for tooling will increase over the next five years as we develop supplier bases to support our products. That is why it is essential to have a Supplier Certification Program in place which seeks to meet the objectives above while reducing the number of suppliers.

The early stages of involvement in JIT Purchasing will require some organizational changes. For example, companies will start to put Buyer/Planner concepts into place. We firmly believe that the more people involved in supporting JIT Purchasing, the higher the success rate. And it must begin with support for change on top management's part.

CHAPTER 11: Case Studies

The following case studies are all derived from actual work done at clients of Professionals for Technology Associates, Inc. (PRO-TECH), an international management counseling and education firm, and from discussions with people knowledgeable in the area of JIT manufacturing. We have attempted to select companies of varying sizes and types in order to give a representative sample of American manufacturing. We have also selected companies and people to whom we could pose questions which are uppermost in the minds of company managers. These are questions about real situations. We have selected companies like yours and people like you and asked a series of questions we think you would want answered.

Mereen Johnson Machine Co.
Minneapolis, MN

DATA: Mereen Johnson manufactures high-production machine tools for the wood processing industry in such areas as windows and doors. In business for over 80 years, the company now has sales of approximately $15 million and employs 230 people.

QUESTION: What are the benefits of Just-In-Time for smaller companies?

ANSWER: When President Russ McBroom is asked about the benefits of JIT for smaller companies, his answer has one common theme — involvement. Two particular areas are foremost in McBroom's mind. They are building partnerships with suppliers and involving employees in company improvement. He is hard pressed to identify either area as more important than the other. To him, the improvement of supplier relations is the major benefit of JIT, but employee involvement is the means by which he can reach his ends.

Smaller companies, he explains, often don't have the clout with suppliers that larger companies have. To offset this disadvantage, Mereen Johnson did business with a number of suppliers to insure delivery of quality material. But this created a situation in which it was necessary to maintain control over an ever increasing supplier base. This is hardly a desirable situation. Once Mereen Johnson began their JIT program, however, McBroom found that the "less suppliers we had, the better our business relationships were with the suppliers we kept."

"We could do better business," McBroom says, "because they got to know our product better and were able to make suggestions to us about how to design and manufacture less expensive and higher quality products."

But none of this will be possible without a Supplier Certification program which insures process control at the supplier's plant. And, as we have seen, a strong and trusting relationship between supplier and purchaser is imperative for reaching the goal where a supplier is an involved member of a JIT team.

When Mereen Johnson began their JIT program in July 1987, McBroom says that the company had two goals in mind. One was to improve employee involvement and, two was to eliminate obsolete and surplus inventory.

"Employee involvement is important," McBroom says, "because that is how we get all the rest of the work done."

McBroom goes on to say that employee involvement "improved substantially" after the JIT program began. The reason why is also the answer to what is the most important component of program implementation — forming teams to address specific problems. McBroom cites a welding operation which took over one day to complete. He now says that employees are able to complete two such operations in one shift. Further more, there has been a substantial increase in quality as well. Prior to set-up reduction of the welding operation, weldments were often sent back and forth between the welding and machining shop because the welding was done incorrectly. Now, every part leaving the welding shop is "100% right." McBroom also notes that the improvements made in quality and set-up time will allow Mereen Johnson to have better control over inventory.

What delights McBroom the most is that all of this improvement was a direct result of JIT project teams. In fact, for the example above, all of the ideas for set-up reduction were generated by production employees. One member of the production crew even did the fixture drawings which made possible the reduction in set-up time.

What makes JIT project teams so effective? At Mereen Johnson, McBroom knows it is because the teams are "structured across departments and levels of employees." In other words, involvement.

"At Mereen Johnson, involvement is infectious," says C.J. Long, senior vice president of PRO-TECH. "Having worked with Russ, I am impressed by his commitment to what he says. When he asks his people to get involved, he leads the way by becoming involved himself."

General Foods Corp.
Dover Facility

DATA: General Food's Dover facility produces dried packaged foods such as jell-o, puddings and Stovetop Stuffing. The plant, one of the largest food producers in the United States, has been in operation for over 23 years. Currently, the facility covers 26 acres and employs 1,100 people.

QUESTION: How does one implement JIT in a large corporation?

ANSWER: Before answering the question, Plant Manager Dick Chalfant wanted to clear up any misconceptions about JIT.

"JIT is a much broader concept than working capital or inventory reduction," he said. "It requires understanding up and down the organization and it requires commitment."

In other words, implementing JIT, whether it is in a large

corporation or a smaller one, is based on education and training coupled with management commitment. Chalfant admits that it is "hard to turn on a dime" when you are large, but not so difficult when you prepare people to participate. Referring to the union people in his own plant, he applauds the fact that there was "lots of participation even though people were learning to do their jobs differently."

Chalfant uses the Ford Motor Co. as an example of another large corporation which was able to turn itself around. Unlike General Motors, which thought it could buy a solution to improve quality, Ford "started at the grass roots level." Chalfant believes that Ford succeeded because it listened to consumer responses, because it encouraged the support of its workers and, most importantly, because it was committed to the long haul.

"American industry all too often thinks that it can solve a problem with time and money by next Wednesday," Chalfant says. "But there is no short-term fix. We need longer commitments to improvement. We need tenacity."

Right now, American industry tends to have a quarterly or annual outlook which is even reflected in its ubiquitous annual performance reviews, Chalfant notes. Until we can think in longer terms, we will not be able to make long-term commitments.

"JIT Purchasing takes this extra step," Chalfant continues. "It builds better supplier partnerships by extending the terms of the contract. We make three-year contracts with our people and unions. Why not with our suppliers? With that type of commitment from us, they can make investements in improving their own performance."

It is obvious that Chalfant has understood the need to be committed and the need to seek and encourage the participation of partners whether they be plant workers or suppliers.

Computervision Corporation
Manchester, N.H.

DATA: Computervison is a developer of CAD/CAM/CAE

hardware and software. The corporation has sales of approximately $560 million. The Manchester plant, which has been in operation for seven years, employs 250 people. The corporation employs approximately 4,500.

QUESTION: How does bar coding interact with JIT Purchasing? What are some of the applications?

ANSWER: Walter Merrill, Plant Materials Manager, sees bar coding as an extremely important communication link in the JIT environment.

"It is the ultimate link between humans, materials and machines," he says.

Merrill also believes the applications of bar coding in JIT Purchasing extend far beyond increased speed and data accuracy of data entry and material tracking. He lists the following applications as obtainable by all companies willing to commit themselves to the effort:

ELECTRONICS INDUSTRY
APPLICATIONS OF BAR CODE

- Supplier Participation (Bar Code Material Shipments)
- Material Tracking (Receiving, Stockrooms, Work-In-Process)
- Quality Defects Analysis
- Capital Assets Identification
- Shipping Documentation
- Physical Inventories/Cycle Counts
- Distribution Centers
- Field Service
- Employee Badge Identification
- Pal/Prom Control
- Q/C Inspections

"As for JIT Purchasing," Merrill continues, "the most critical area is supplier participation. We begin by educating our suppliers about bar coding objectives. Then we supply them with labels at first and show them how and where to apply them.

"We move gradually until all suppliers comply. I think this is the key to our success. We don't impose our system on them. We work with our suppliers in a partnership."

The results are truly impressive. Computervision's facility is a clean, organized and pleasant workplace. The complete material flow is tracked via bar code from the receiving dock to the shipping dock. Information is fed into the facility's on-line materials system as material flows through inspection, testing, stockroom, kitting and work-in-process. Bar code labels are applied to parts or boxes of parts so that they will either be stored or sent to the appropriate point on the production line. Labels also identify where each product is in the assembly process. For example, it is possible to know that Thursday's shipment of sheet metal is now in the paint shop because the label contains receiving information.

What information a label contains is, of course, subject to some limitations, but how it is used is only subject to your imagination. Bar coding supports MRP and MRP II which, in turn, forms a base for JIT. Computervision utilizes the ASK MAN/MAN manufacturing resource planning system on a fully integrated basis. Such coordinated information is vital to the attainment of the ultimate JIT goal — the right material in the right place at the right time.

Cosmair, Inc.
Division of L'Oréal
Piscataway, New Jersey

DATA: Cosmair is a consumer commodities supplier of cosmetics, hair care products, and fragrances. Sales for 1988 are expected to be between $970-975 million.

QUESTION: How does a person at the executive level instill a sense of management commitment in a company? How does that person deal with the people who work at the company?

ANSWER: "I think these questions are at the heart of JIT," says Gerry Price, Assistant Vice President of Manufacturing at Cosmair, Inc. "And I mean 'heart' in two senses — as the vital core that pumps health and life into a company and as the vessel of understanding. That brings me right into the second part of the question — how do you deal with people?

"You can't go in and change the way a company operates with just management commitment. It has to start there, but it won't work if you don't put some of the human heart into it."

Management commitment thus means a commitment to listening to the people who work for you. Of course, there is always the possibility that when you open up meetings to free and open discourse, they will turn non-productive as participants accuse and criticize. Criticism is fine, but it must be constructive; it must pertain to the object of the discussion, not to personal problems. Again, management commitment is important here as well.

"Management must be committed to education and training," says Price. "We firmly believe that the whole company should know what JIT is about and then they should be trained in problem-solving techniques so that they can employ their JIT education.

"From the beginning, however, we promised ourselves that education was as important at the executive and management level as it was at the worker level, perhaps more important. We wanted to avoid the situation where one of our people would become frustrated because management only received a two-hour briefing on JIT. That happens. Managers don't have time to learn theory, they say. At Cosmair, we feel differently. It's where education starts and with education comes understanding, not only of the concepts of JIT, but also of the people side of JIT."

Truck-Lite Co., Inc.
Falconer, New York

DATA: Truck-Lite manufactures vehicle safety lighting for the automotive and OEM heavy-duty industries. The company has sales of approximately $40 million.

QUESTION: What is the role of Purchasing in the JIT environment?

ANSWER: "At Truck-Lite," says Purchasing Manager Wayne Revenew, "the role of Purchasing starts with getting suppliers certified. Through certification, we then aim for just-in-time delivery of materials from our suppliers."

Revenew also recognizes that reaching the goal of JIT delivery and supplier certification also requires new approaches internal to his company. For example, he cites production control and the need for more accurate forecasting. The logic is quite simple, he feels. With control over production, his company's forecasts for production schedules will be far more accurate. Accurate estimates of production schedules will then make for accurate estimates of material needs, both in terms of quantity and delivery dates. If you can provide suppliers with accurate quantities and delivery dates, he reasons, then they are more able to control their own production schedules so that they can deliver just-in-time.

"JIT Purchasing won't work without an internal and external component," he concludes. "Besides our work certifying suppliers, we have engaged upon an MRP II program. We have hired a full-time trainer whose job it is to assist Purchasing in restructuring so that it can take advantage of Manufacturing Resource Planning."

As for the supplier side, Revenew is a member of a Purchased Parts Management Team which is comprised of six to seven members. Each member in turn heads another team, such as Awards, Supplier Consolidation, Parts Consolidation, Manuals and Supplier Certification which Revenew refers to as the "hit team."

"These are the people," he explains, " who are directly involved with the suppliers. They go into a supplier's company and present an action plan for implementing a certification program. They establish a format and schedule for the program and monitor the supplier's progress. All this material is contained in a manual which we put together on Supplier Certification. We also prepare a Quality Control manual to accompany it."

Revenew is pleased with the progress made so far by Truck-Lite. Recently, his company certified a supplier who delivers over 30 parts. This took four to five months, but Revenew considers it time well spent. Now, it's as though the two companies speak the same language, having cleared up all blueprint discrepancies as well as established process controls.

"Our next goal," says Revenew, "is to get suppliers to ship JIT. We are aiming for a three-day window on both sides of the due date. This will be a considerable improvement over the past and will greatly improve our control."

Paul Hine, CPM
Education Chairman, Connecticut Chapter
National Association of Purchasing Management

Director of Materials, Dual-Lite Company
Newtown, CT

DATA: Dual-Lite is the number one manufacturer of emergency indoor lighting in the country. Its products are found in commercial lighting and exit signs.

QUESTION: What is the thrust of JIT in Purchasing?

ANSWER: "It is clear," says Paul Hine, CPM, "that JIT is gaining increasing momentum, but not always in the best manner. Too often, pressure is being placed on Purchasing to push material onto the supplier instead of seeing JIT as a way to improve internal conditions.

"Dumping inventory on suppliers is not JIT," he continues. "Those companies who see JIT this way have not been educated properly. I see the growing movement toward JIT as existing on a spectrum. At one end are the companies who dump inventory. At the other end are the companies who are working with their suppliers and cleaning up internal problems."

If education is the key to understanding and implementing JIT correctly, then how does one get educated? Hine says the first step is to attend seminars and workshops which give overviews of JIT as well as more specific areas such as Supplier Certification. Hine calls these "enlightenment seminars." Their purpose is to make participants see that JIT is more than inventory control, but a means whereby one can improve one's own company.

Hine cites the case of one supplier for Dual-Lite who, two years ago, did not even monitor their delivery performance.

"Now, they are proud of their near-perfect adherence to due dates," says Hine. "They now use it as an excellent selling tool for their company."

After enlightenment comes implementation through a formal or informal supplier certification program, Hine explains. But, this can't be done without resolving quality questions.

"How can a supplier expect to deliver JIT, if it can't produce quality parts? And how can a company receiving the parts expect true JIT capability, if it has no control over their internal production and delivered goods sit in receiving or warehouses instead of being shipped directly to the line?

"Education is a two-way street," Hine says. "You learn as much as you teach."

Cosmair, Inc.
Designer Fragrance Division
North Brunswick, New Jersey

DATA: Cosmair is a consumer commodities supplier of cosmetics, hair care products, and fragrances. Sales for 1988 are expected to be between $970-975 million. There are approximately 55-60 support people working in the Designer Fragrance Division at North Brunswick.

QUESTION: How important is top management commitment to the success of JIT Purchasing? And how does it translate into action?

ANSWER: "Top management commitment is everything," says Fred Hoffman, Director of Manufacturing Services at Cosmair's Designer Fragrance Division. He should know because when his division began a JIT implementation, he was named the JIT Coordinator. Thus, he has been witness to top management's first movements toward the new program.

"At Cosmair," he says, "top management gave us a clear direction and the latitude and resources to make it happen. This was about two years ago. We realized right from the start that our success was contingent upon thoroughly understanding the concepts of JIT. Upon this educational foundation, we would implement the program."

Prior to this step, however, Cosmair's top management had made another commitment to becoming a world-class competitor by structuring their organization around specific classes of trade. Each of these trade divisions consisted of a manufacturing and customer care or distribution part. The idea was to make each division into a focus factory of 125-150 people. The Division Vice President was essentially a plant manager. Under the VP were Directors in such areas as Purchasing, Planning, Manufacturing Services, etc. Staff at the corporate level of Cosmair supported the divisions in areas like Management Information Systems, Corporate Purchasing, Engineering, etc.

At Cosmair, then, there already was an environment where top management could expect VP's, directors, managers, supervisors and workers to take the responsibility and authority to make things happen. This is what happened for the JIT project. The vice president of the division and the directors, about five or six people, started attending workshops and reading publications and books to acquaint themselves with the whole area. As it became necessary, they took workshops in specific areas like Statistical Process Control, Inventory Record Accuracy or Supplier Certification to augment the total educational process.

Hoffman found that the varied backgrounds of the people involved in this educational process were highly benficial. Each person contributed in the area of their discipline, thus creating a synergistic whole.

Now, the group needed a coordinator to supervise the JIT implementation and develop a training program for all the people working at the plant.

"Our overall strategy was to tell people where we were heading and why," says Hoffman. "We selected a training program of 12 videotapes which dealt with areas like change-over times, quality and so on. We divided the plant into groups of 10 people and went through the entire video program with each. That meant everybody, from clerk typists to supervisors to managers."

"From the start," Hoffman continues, "we saw that we first had to concentrate on our basic business instead of our promotional business for holidays like Christmas or Mother's Day."

Hoffman's project team then attacked the area of supplier certification by drawing up criteria and a schedule. The team then selected five to seven suppliers and worked with them to develop a better relationship — sharing production requirements, annualized needs and simplified specifications.

The results of JIT implementation were gratifying. Hoffman says that inventory accuracy improved from 70% to 99+%. They have maintained this level for over two years. In fact, Hoffman says, they are now exempt from physical inventories. In inventory reduction, Hoffman reports that the plant has gone from storing material on four to five thousand pallets to between two and two-and-a-half thousand. Or, a reduction of approximately 50%.

"We haven't finished yet," says Hoffman. "Our next step is quality. We want to get our suppliers into the Statistical Process Control mentality. We want to have data from their manufacturing operations so that we know our shipments are not only arriving on time, but are free of defects. Then we can lower our inventory buffers even further."

Hoffman attributes the success of the JIT program at his plant to the mutual cooperation between groups.

"You can get that cooperation when there are fewer people and fewer levels of management," he says.

In other words, top management's commitment to the focus factory and to allocating responsibility and authority has helped to assure the success of JIT.

Newell Window Furnishings Company
Freeport, IL.

DATA: Newell is a manufacturer of drapery hardware (curtain rods, traverse rods, etc.), window shades, mini-blinds, rollups and shower rods. In business for 70 years, the facility employs 510 people and has annual sales of $70 million.

QUESTION: What are the overall goals and objectives of the executive level in establishing and supporting a JIT project team? How should executives work with such a team in order to produce results? What is the importance of "leader speaks last" (LSL)?

ANSWER: In answering the question of what are the goals and objectives of a JIT team, Brett D. Hoyt, Vice President of Operations, gave the following list:

- Elimination of waste and inefficiencies
- Involve employees at all levels
- Listen to problems and concerns of people on floor
- Support (in word and action) the recommendations and directions of JIT teams
- Allow and encourage production personnel to visit and communicate with suppliers
- Improve customer service and satisfaction
- Treat everyone as an equal

Hoyt and his fellow vice presidents, as well as the president of Newell, often attend WOW (War on Waste) meetings. Hoyt also believes in spreading the gospel of JIT beyond the company.

"We sent a team of ten employees, including five production workers to a supplier in Chicago to review their processes, quality, people and commitment to Newell. The production workers did most of the talking and communicated Newell's goals and philosophy with regard to our WOW program."

Hoyt says that he is directly involved in the Hot Rodders WOW team. As a vice president, he feels that he can help make the team work best by attending all the meetings and by treating everyone as an equal.

"Mostly I keep quiet," he says, "only using my pencil to jot down ideas and information. I do offer support as needed, but mostly I listen. The best way I can help our team get results is by supporting their recommendations, by offering to serve on a subcommittee to provide information and by contacting other personnel within the company and asking for their support.

"At Newell, we also try to give recognition to those who have contributed. We offer training dollars and pay for extra work done by production workers."

And Hoyt is committed himself. When his company wisited the Chicago supplier mentioned above, he drove his own van.

As for the policy of LSL ("leader speaks last"), Hoyt believes that when a leader dominates the conversation, it stifles innovation and involvement from others.

"They think that this is a management program and that they are there to watch. People want to be heard, but only if management's interest is genuine and not just lip service.

"We had a case where one of our production workers spoke out against WOW because he thought higher wages were guaranteed with the installation of the program. Instead of stifling his comments, I listened with everyone else and, at the end, expressed my thanks that he took the risk and shared his feelings. I also promised to get back to the group with the actual numbers and some overviews, which I did."

Hoyt says that the production worker's point was well taken and indeed his earnings had gone down. But they had not gone down due to the WOW program, but because of an incentive rate change and increased downtime due to machine problems.

"We are now addressing and resolving those machine problems and the worker is satisfied that he got a fair shake from the company and that we let him speak out."

This policy of LSL, coupled with Hoyt's practice of frequently visiting the floor, has done much to convince people that he is part of their team.

"Following up to their questions is vital," Hoyt says. "And the rewards for doing so are great. Production personnel begin to trust you and relate to you if you get back to them promptly about their concerns."

General Foods Corp.
Dover Facility

DATA: General Food's Dover facility produces dried packaged foods such as jell-o, puddings and Stovetop Stuffing. The plant, one of the largest food producers in the United States, has been in operation for over 23 years. Currently, the facility covers 26 acres and employs 1100 people.

QUESTION: How do you implement JIT in a large company?

ANSWER: Ed Gazze, Manager of Operations Systems Dry Deserts, says that the first step in achieving JIT Purchasing is to "avoid the temptation of going directly to vendors and saying 'you must do this' or 'you will do that'."

To avoid this temptation meant first understanding the company's purchasing and supply chain better and secondly getting the company's own operations better organized.

"We had to understand how our own methods of operation were contributing to the effectiveness or ineffectiveness of our purchasing function," says Gazze. "Our goal was to effectively supply our plant with the right amount of usable materials at the right time."

Gazze said there were several symptoms which led the company to explore a Just-In-Time approach to its Purchasing/Material Supply System:

- Frequent out-of-stocks.
- Incidents of materials which would not perform on equipment (even though they were within specification).
- Stock status on inventory which was not timely or up-to-date.
- Vendors delivering materials too early or too late.

Once the symtoms were identified, the company decided to from a team to find their real causes. As project manager for this team, Gazze met with each functional department manager to get their input as to the make-up of the team. Eventually, the team consisted of hourly and salaried personnel and several key managers from Logistics, Warehouse and Finance.

"The team met every other week," says Gazze, " to investigate the key factors influencing effective purchasing and material supply. After much discussion in which the team employed cause and effect (fishbone) diagrams, we chose to work on the area of record accuracy since we believed it was the most significant factor."

The team's first hurdle was finding the right measurements to determine how accurate their current reporting system was. Gazze said that they initially believed that their system was 75-80% accurate.To see if they were right, they implemented cycle counting. Before they could use the system, however, the plant had to be educated and trained in its use.

"The team arranged and prepared education and training programs for material handlers, supervisors, clerks, buyers and production employees involved in the purchasing system," Gazze reports. "The program was assisted by hourly workers and supervisors who had demonstrated in their daily work a high regard for accurate material accounting."

The cycle counting then began. A group of two people started counting a portion of the warehouse daily and reconciled their count with the stock status.

"The initial findings were shocking," says Gazze. "We had a 42% accuracy level."

Instead of being discouraged, the team saw this as an opportunity to follow up on the variations until the cause of the error was established. Using Pareto analysis, the team categorized the causes and began to resolve them one-by-one.

"In 15 weeks, the accuracy improvement was dramatic,"Gazze reports. "It went up to 88%. Twelve weeks later it reached 92%. We also found that the symptoms we had identified earlier began to be reduced. Stock outs, for example, went from once every three days to once every nine days."

With the accuracy vastly improved, buyers were able to effectively work with vendors on managing deliveries. Inventories were cut back for all products. For example, the team was able to eliminate 30,000 cases kept on hand for a packaging operation. This cut had no impact on productivity and resulted in no stock outs.

The team's success soon rippled through the plant. Building on their experience tackling record accuracy, the team began to tackle other material management problems such as quality and count of arriving materials. They have also started to work on deciding which suppliers could and should be part of a Supplier Certification program.

While studying accuracy, the team discovered that material identification was not standardized. A team was spun off to develop a standardized material handling program. They have succeeded to the extent that they are now working with Corporate Purchasing to implement the program throughout the corporation.

Another team was spun off to improve the timeliness and quality of information from Logistics and Systems functions. The effect this has had on purchasing and material control has been dramatic as well. Gazze reports inventory reductions on the order of 40-50% for some materials.

Perhaps most importantly, however, the JIT team helped to break down the functional roles between management and labor.

"Both sides are working freely together to resolve a problem," Gazze says, " rather than deciding which side of the problem they are on. The JIT team has definitely provided a model for a worker/ management partnership instead of a management only direction.

Progressive Technology Inc.
Rocky Hill, CT

DATA: Founded in 1950, Progressive Technology Inc. (PTI) is a precision machine shop specializing in experimental and prototype work for the computer, aerospace, defense and commercial industries.

QUESTION: How does one implement JIT in a machine shop environment?

ANSWER: . Since this machine shop had never been operated on the principles of JIT before, Ralph Williams, General Manager, found that training and education were his number one priorities.

He stresses three areas as critical:

- Quality as the responsibility of each operator.
- Institution of basic scheduling techniques.
- Presence of a teamwork mentality.

"Fortunately," says Williams, "we inherited people who believe strongly in quality. Doing work for the computer and aerospace industry over the years has made our operators into people who believe in doing it right the first time. Therefore, our first major hurdle had already been cleared.

"Next we instituted some simple daily and weekly schedules, a master schedule and shop loading. Since everything we build is unique, there is a great need for coordination which is flexible. Already, we are able to receive daily deliveries from suppliers, put the material into work-in-process and then ship it out the door as soon as the product is completed. We operate in a virtually zero inventory environment."

This achievement was possible, Williams says, because teamwork extends beyond the four walls of PTI. Teamwork must not only exist in a plant but with the company's suppliers and customers.

"Success," says Williams, "depends upon people of different skills, disciplines and functions working together to achieve the mutual goal of quality parts, on time and at competitive prices. This is what JIT strives for. This striving is based upon a respect for each player's contribution, open communication and a willingness to place the success of the team above self-interest."

Now that a base has been built upon, Williams says he is ready to begin JIT training. But he feels that constructing the base was the most important step. That base, he says, is a commitment to excellence. It is also the philosophy of PRO-TECH which recently acquired Progressive Technology. According to Williams, the purchase gives PRO-TECH an opportunity "to put into practice what they preach."

"To us," he concludes, "a commitment to excellence is the backbone of JIT and the same thing as survival."

Conclusion

There is one predominant conclusion to this chapter and this book — we *can* achieve excellence here in America. The companies in the preceeding case studies are testimony to that fact. Purchasing has played a prominent role in these rebirths. There are no tricks, just hard work and a commitment which permeates all levels of your company. As you start pursuing excellence in your own JIT Purchasing program, you will find that this rule applies to all companies whatever your size or product. You will also find that the desire to search for the true causes of problems accompanies this commitment. Remember, however, that commitment does not come without partnerships between you and your suppliers as well as between you and the people who work with you at your company. Like we said, there is no mystery to excellence. Those who master an art or a sport have achieved thepursuit of excellencethrough many hours of study and practice. Manufacturers who wish to achieve mastery can expect to do no less.

REFERENCES

Chapter One

(1) Peter L. Grieco, Jr., Michael W. Gozzo, *MADE IN AMERICA: The Total Business Concept,* PT Publications, Inc., Plantsville, CT, p. 4, 1987.

Chapter Two

(1) Lamar Lee, Jr., Donald W. Dobler, *Purchasing and Materials Management: Text and Cases*, McGraw-Hill Book Company, New York, p. 20, 1977.

(2) Lamar Lee, Jr., Donald W. Dobler, *Purchasing and Materials Management: Text and Cases*, McGraw-Hill Book Company, New York, p. 20-21, 1977.

(3) Erik Sandberg-Diment, "The Invoice Is in the Ether," *The New York Times*, p. 18, Mar. 22, 1987.

(4) James B. Morgan, "How to deal with pricing without having it dominate the activity," *Purchasing Magazine*, p.33, Feb. 13, 1986.

(5) James B. Morgan, "How to deal with pricing without having it dominate the activity," *Purchasing Magazine*, p.33, Feb. 13, 1986.

Chapter Three

(1) Peter L. Grieco, Jr., Michael W. Gozzo, *MADE IN AMERICA: The Total Business Concept,* PT Publications, Inc., Plantsville, CT, p. 182, 1987.

(2) Walter Merrill, "Bar Coding in the Electronics Industry," *Bar Code News*, p. 42.

(3) Debra Marshall, "Quick Pick," *ID Systems*, p. 36, May 1987.

(4) Walter Merrill, "Bar Coding in the Electronics Industry," *Bar Code News*, p. 42.

(5) Walter Merrill, "Bar Coding in the Electronics Industry," *Bar Code News*, p. 42.

Chapter Four

(1) W. Edwards Deming, *Quality, Productivity and Competitive Position,* MIT Center for Advanced Engineering Study, Cambridge, MA, 1982.

Chapter Five

(1) Lamar Lee, Jr., Donald W. Dobler, *Purchasing and Materials Management: Text and Cases*, McGraw-Hill Book Company, New York, p. 13, 1977.

(2) Lamar Lee, Jr., Donald W. Dobler, *Purchasing and Materials Management: Text and Cases*, McGraw-Hill Book Company, New York, p. 256, 1977.

(3) Lamar Lee, Jr., Donald W. Dobler, *Purchasing and Materials Management: Text and Cases*, McGraw-Hill Book Company, New York, p. 257, 1977.

(4) Somerby Dowst CPM, "Better Forged links bring in better designs:purchasing's enhanced position in the information loop maximizes suppliers' engineering assistance," *Purchasing Magazine*, p. 67, Sept. 6, 1984.

(5) Somerby Dowst CPM, "Better Forged links bring in better designs:purchasing's enhanced position in the information loop maximizes suppliers' engineering assistance," *Purchasing Magazine*, p. 73, Sept. 6, 1984.

(6) Lamar Lee, Jr., Donald W. Dobler, *Purchasing and Materials Management: Text and Cases*, McGraw-Hill Book Company, New York, p. 131, 1977.

(7) Peter L. Grieco, Jr., Michael W. Gozzo, *MADE IN AMERICA: The Total Business Concept,* PT Publications, Inc., Plantsville, CT, p. 174-175, 1987.

Chapter Six

(1) H. Thomas Johnson and Robert S. Kaplan, *Relevance Lost: The Rise and Fall of Management Accounting*, Harper & Row, New York, 1987.

(2) Richard C. Wadleigh, "What's your excuse for not using JIT?," *Harvard Business Review*, p. 42, Mar-Apr 1986.

(3) Richard C. Wadleigh, "What's your excuse for not using JIT?," *Harvard Business Review*, p. 42, March-April 1986.

Chapter Seven

None.

Chapter Eight

(1) Larry Engelmann and Michael Malone, "Controlling the Current Chaos," *American Way*, p. 10-15, 1988.

Chapter Nine

(1) Paul Hoffman, "The Man Who Loves Only Numbers," *The Atlantic Monthly*, p. 60-73, Nov. 1987.
(2) Noboru Ibi, "Toyota's Creative Suggestion System," *InSite*, P.D.S. International Ltd., Tokyo, Japan, p 20-27, Jan. 1988.
(3) Noboru Ibi, "Toyota's Creative Suggestion System," *InSite*, P.D.S. International Ltd., Tokyo, Japan, p 20-27, Jan. 1988.

Chapter Ten

(1) Russell Mitchell, "When Jack Welch Takes Over: A Guide for the Newly Acquired," *Business Week*, p. 95, Dec. 14, 1987.

Chapter Eleven

None.

ANSWERS

TQC — Total Quality Control
WIP — Work-In-Process
VAP — Vendors as Partners
ZI — Zero Inventory
CIP — Continuous Improvement Program
5Ws — Why? Why? Why? Why? Why?
SMED — Single Minute Exchange of Die
FFU — Fitness for Use
ZD — Zero Defect
OTC — One Touch Changeover
DSE — Different Set of Eyes
LSL — Leader Speaks Last
ESP — Employee Suggestion Programs
MBWA — Management By Walking Around
SLP — Small Lot Production
MMP — Mixed Model Production
LLP — Level Load Production
SPC — Statistical Process Control
CED — Cause and Effect Diagrams
TPM — Total Preventive Maintenance

INDEX